# Happiness and Success

### Evidence-Based Strategies for Success.

## MICHAEL HUNT

authorHOUSE®

*AuthorHouse™*
*1663 Liberty Drive*
*Bloomington, IN 47403*
*www.authorhouse.com*
*Phone: 1 (800) 839-8640*

*Published by AuthorHouse    03/04/2016*

*ISBN: 978-1-5049-8162-0 (sc)*
*ISBN: 978-1-5049-8161-3 (e)*

**Client and business testimonials:**

*"Your coaching and thoughtful guidance has been absolutely critical in turning my life around for the better. I'm extremely grateful!!!!"*

John M
Resort Manager
Los Angeles, CA, USA

*"I find working with Michael very empowering and this collaboration is really helping me enormously to move forward in my life. Michael is a wonderful, highly recommended coach who supports me in my self-development and in reaching for my highest aspiration and goals."*

Sahara
Workshop Facilitator
London, England

*"Michael is supportive, insightful, and engaging"*

Ashley
Massachusetts, USA

*"I have known Michael for many years, watching his journey with great interest and admiration. Not only is he insightful, knowledgeable, and truly understands the concepts of success and happiness, but he lives by them, allowing him and his family to live an extraordinary life."*

Mark Morris
Managing Director
M2 Design and Construction
Melbourne, Australia

*"I had the privilege of working for and with Michael for 5 years in Brisbane, Australia. Michael is extremely approachable, insightful, and supportive. For the years I worked with Michael, I looked at him as a mentor and the wealth of*

*knowledge and willingness to help others and share his thoughts with everyone in a positive way was inspiring and empowering."*

Michelle McCuaig
Operations Manager
Brisbane. Australia

*"Having known Michael for many years both as a work colleague and a friend, I have found Michael's commitment to work and life an inspiration. Michael not only helps many people with his coaching, he lives the fundamentals in his own life with great success."*

Nathan Smith
Account Manager
Melbourne, Australia.

*"When I need love, I talk to my wife.*
*When I want answers, I talk to God.*
*But, when I need motivation - Mike is the man!"*

James Maclean
Owner/Manager, Express English
Izmir, Turkey

# Contents

# Introduction

*"For things to remain the same, everything must change"*
*Giuseppe di Lampedusa, The Leopard, 1960*

Have you ever thought about what really makes you happy? And how does this relate to your success? At times, both aspects seem mutually exclusive. We sacrifice our happiness for success. At times, we work long hours and/or do jobs we do not love, all so we have resources to then be happy. As common as this is, it turns out there is a better way.

Are you happy in your career or job? Maybe for you, like I found, there are parts of your job that you like and parts you don't like. I spent 20 years managing, mentoring staff, and running telecommunications/IT projects. I ran an office and I dealt with all kinds of different clients. In retrospect, although I liked my job overall, it was very difficult for me to start to identify the parts of my job that I liked the most. As it turned out, although I started as an engineer and have always been very technical, what I loved the most about my job was the personal interaction. Connecting with and helping others was what I really enjoyed. This took me a long time to realise. Looking back now, it was obvious. That's why I moved from my engineering role into service delivery, operations management, and ultimately, into projects and office management roles.

Isn't it interesting, looking back and thinking about how our career and our personal life have progressed? Sometimes, change is forced upon us, sometimes it just happens, and sometimes we lean towards the work we enjoy and end up doing that. This is what happened to me. As I climbed the corporate ladder, I found that I was using my intrapersonal skills more and more. As time went on, I relied less on my skills as an engineer and more on my "soft skills," as they call them in the industry.

Lucky for me, the more time I spent helping my engineers in personal and work challenges, the better they performed and the more successful my projects were. This often was the case with my clients and other stakeholders.

The stronger our relationships, the more I could help them in their work and sometimes personal life. This leads to more successful projects and a better office environment. It wasn't until I took a break from my career in the corporate world that I could truly take a step back and appreciate all that had happened. I began to discover with increasing confidence that my true calling, my real passion in life was about helping people. Not only helping people who are struggling through personal or work issues, but also helping people achieve and succeed in what's really important to them.

If I could do just one thing for you, it would be to give you the ability to reassess and re-evaluate your work and your personal life to find out what you are really passionate about. What do you really love about the work you are doing now? What do you most enjoy within your personal life and what can you do to take full advantage of this passion?

This is the real key to happiness and success.

The good news is that we have been born in an extremely unique time in human evolution. When I was at school, we did not even have a computer room. We could not Google the answers to some of the most complex questions in our lives. We could not access the wisdom and knowledge from the ages. Today, we have an unprecedented access to information which only a few decades ago was unavailable; information from researchers, philosophers and the great thinkers of our time.

In my career change from Program Manager to Life Coach, I was surprised to find how easily accessible research papers and study results were. Professors and philosophers who have spent their lives studying the key to happiness and success have written detailed research papers outlining their findings from their experiments and real life studies. They have handed us the answer to how we can be happy and successful in our lives on a silver platter. Of course, some of these research papers and studies can be very dry reading. Fortunately for you, over the last two years, I have read and tried to understand the learnings from hundreds of these studies. I present to you, within the pages of this book, the true essence of their findings. I combine their findings with my own personal experience; firstly, in the corporate world, then in coaching and training individuals in their lifestyle changes and of course my own life experiences. In my coaching I have helped people who have been unemployed for a long time find a job. I have assisted clients to set up charities, rediscover their own passions, build their motivation and productivity in their work, and many other individual personal successes.

I aim to build your passion around what is really meaningful in your life, so you can explore the possibilities and the opportunities in your life that may not seem immediately obvious. Personally, I find it amazing that we live in this time of human history. James Cook only arrived in Australia 250 years ago, although humans have been walking around the planet for 40,000 years. We are in a period of transformation on this tiny blue planet, some 40,000 billion kilometres away from any other possible habitable land. Never in the history of human existence, on this little speck within the cosmos, have we ever had a better opportunity to be happy and successful than right now.

As you read this book, please understand the research that tells us that 40% of our own happiness can be controlled directly from our own perspective and the way we interact with our world. Only 10% of our happiness is dependent on our wealth and our personal situation, such as a nice house or car. This in itself should tell us we need to reassess the priorities we put on financial success. The other half of our happiness is controlled by our genetics. This in itself is not all bad. Do you have a grumpy friend or relative who was just born to be unhappy? You may notice that sometimes this person can actually be quite happy deep down. We are all born with a generic range of happiness. That range may be between a little happy and extremely happy, or extremely unhappy and just living. The fact is, when we are living at the top of our own personal genetic range of happiness, we feel alive, we are loving life and everything is good, regardless of the perception of others.

So please, enjoy this book. Have fun with it and appreciate the unique opportunity that you have right now to be happy and successful. Relate it all to your own personal experience. Ask yourself how this can help you in your own journey towards happiness and success. How you can be energised within this experience of expanding possibilities to live a flourishing life. Let yourself be inspired to live a meaningful, happy, and successful life. Now is the time to explore the limitless possibilities within this perfect storm of human evolution, on this tiny speck within the cosmos. Take advantage of the ancient wisdom and the knowledge that is being painstakingly documented and researched over generations. This knowledge, that now, through the newly connected global community, we are able to access.

# Acknowledgments

In writing this book, I studied many research papers, books, and delved into my own experiences. I would like to acknowledge the work of Martin E. P. Seligman for his extensive research and knowledge of positive psychology. Shawn Achor, for all his work on success through happiness in the workplace. Barbara Fredrickson for her broaden-and-build theory and other research. Sonja Lyubomirsky, Laura King, and Ed Diener, for their meta-analysis study showing how happiness precedes success. Anthony Grant for his research on evidence-based coaching principles. These researchers have dedicated their lives to running tests and studies, and other work that has given us invaluable insights to the workings of ourselves as humans. How we react to different situations and stimuli. What we can do in our lives to receive maximum benefit for the action we take.

Happiness is a catchall phrase that encompasses flourishing, well-being, satisfaction, joy, pleasure, the list goes on. When quoting research, happiness is sometimes substituted when researchers use more technical terms such as high dispositional positive affect, frequent positive affect, positive affect, transient positive affect, and in-dispositional positive affect.

On a more personal note, I would like to thank Adam Freeman for his ongoing support and mentoring, especially around my coaching practice. My clients, who I feel sometimes give me more insight into real life than I give them. My wife Cathy and kids, Dillon, Tom, and Heidi for their support and putting up with me while I wrote this book. My Mum and brothers Dave and Jono, for sharing their real life experience and all their guidance over the years. My extended family; it is amazing how much I have learnt from the Hunt and Woodhouse families. A special mention to my father, Pete, and my sister Susan, who are not around to enjoy this book. Finally, a big thank you to all for taking the time to read this book. I trust you will gain valuable insights into the inner workings of your own mind, what motivates you, how your actions affect your perceived environment and most importantly, how to ensure your life is positive, happy, and successful.

# Chapter 1

# The Big Ship

*"You cannot change your destination overnight, but you can change your direction overnight"*
*Jim Rohn*

We can improve so many things in our lives by making small changes. I want to share the big ship analogy. Think of a big cargo ship powering through the ocean. From the helm, the captain cannot see land. Without the use of instruments, it's very hard to know the specific direction the ship is going. Yet with the tools available, the captain gets to his destination port every time. Throughout the journey, the ship's course is adjusted ever so slightly, over and over again; just like when you're driving a car and the steering wheel doesn't stay still. Even to go straight, you steer a little bit left, then little bit right. The car looks to be going straight, but the wheel is always correcting and compensating.

The ship is the same; there is always a correction of the course, no matter how small. If however, the captain chooses to steer the wheel or pull a lever, ever so slightly the ship will begin to turn. If you are standing on the deck of the ship, staring out to sea, you would not even notice this small change of direction. It may only be a degree or two to the left or to the right.

Without precise instruments to rely on, the ship would appear to be going straight. Over time, as the ship continues to power through the ocean, this small change of direction will make a massive impact. So great is this impact that the ship could end up in a completely different country. A ship bound for England may end up in Africa. When the ship arrives in Africa, the captain and crew face a completely different reality than they originally expected. Life in this different destination is nothing like what they had planned for. At this point, they must decide to offload the cargo

1

and sell it for a fraction of the price they would have received in London, or set sail and travel the 3,500 kilometers north to their original destination.

This massive change of outcome was created by a very small change initially. Our lives work in exactly the same way. Think back to any major achievement or event in your life. Now think of the initial thought, decision, or inspiration that started off the process. Sometimes these just happen, sometimes they are active decisions in response to another situation, or sometimes you have an epiphany! In each way, we see that our life is often directed by very small changes in thoughts and behaviors.

When we first make these decisions or changes, we often don't know the full ramifications of our initial actions. You may get a job, but it was one of 50 others that you applied for. This leads you down the path of a new career choice, skills that you learn, making new friends, or even meeting a partner for life. There are multiple future possible realities that can manifest within every single decision.

In the case of the big ship, it is powering through the ocean regardless of the captain's steering. It is burning through diesel; the crew are maintaining the engines and clearing the decks. There is so much time, money and energy spent to propel the ship through the ocean. Yet the destination of the ship depends on small changes of direction made by the captain.

So too with your life. We already have to get up in the morning and eat breakfast, go to work or play, eat lunch, look after the kids, wash and feed ourselves, sleep and do it all over again. We will always have challenges and issues that we need to overcome. We will always have to motivate ourselves to do what needs to be done. We will always have to deal with our relationships, family, and friends. The energy we use, a bit like the ship, is required no matter what task we devote ourselves to during the day. Without direction, like the ship powering through the ocean, we could end up anywhere. We will still use the time, money, and energy but the destination may not warrant the effort. We may find ourselves selling our cargo at a discounted rate, or having to sail 3,500 kilometers back to our original destination.

*"The goals you set for yourself — like the rudder of a ship — will guide you toward your destination, and without them, like a ship without a rudder, you'll find it impossible to stay the course"*
*The Napoleon Hill Foundation*

One great motivational speaker used to conduct an exercise every time he had a large audience in a workshop or presentation. He would use two volunteers, one would be blindfolded, and the other would stand behind him. He would have them start at one side of the lecture theater and ask the person behind to direct the blindfolded person to a destination on the other side of the auditorium. He was only allowed to give simple directions, such as turn left or turn right. What became obvious is the director, like a driver of a car, or the captain of the ship, would be constantly issuing commands to turn left or to turn right. He was unable to keep the blindfolded man on a straight course without constantly redirecting his direction. This constant banter from the director could easily be perceived negatively. The man with the blindfold was told to turn left, no further left, a little to the right, a little bit more. You can see how annoying this would become if you had a little director sitting on your shoulder through your day-to-day activities and your life. There would be constant banter telling you that you are not going in the right direction. Yet without this constant correction, you may end up at a completely different destination. Then, like our ship, you may spend a lot of time, money, and energy getting back on your original course.

By consistently adjusting our course ever so slightly, we are able to achieve so much more; faster and with greater ease. We are able to achieve our dreams and desires in a fast and efficient way. Through these examples, we are also able to see how a small adjustment in our attitude and perspective has massive consequences, either negative or positive.

*"The power of small changes is much about the importance of time"*
Adam Freeman

These consequences are not always immediately obvious. You may commit to three short runs each week. This may lead you to eating slightly healthier. It may lead you to decide to compete in a 10 km fun run. This could lead to a half marathon or full marathon. Deciding to do a short course at the local college may lead to a career change down the track. This career change could provide many other options in your life, from flexibility in your work environment, to a higher income, that allows you to travel or something similar. Joining the local tennis club, football club, or golf club, even if it is only a once a week commitment, may open you up to a completely different social circle. This social circle can open your eyes to a completely different perspective. Out of this new social circle you may develop lifelong friends, find a partner, discover new interests, or be inspired to take on any number of new challenges. You become aware of the limitless possibilities life has to offer.

We should never underestimate the power of a new direction, interests, or challenges. We should never underestimate how a simple decision may change the rest of our lives. Of course, lack of a decision or a poor decision can have just as extreme negative effect.

This is why it is so important to our happiness and success to have a clear vision and goals in your life. When we know where we want to head and what we need to achieve to get there, the smaller the decisions or adjustments in our steering become easy and natural. They do not feel like constant banter from our self-talk, like someone always telling us to turn left or turn right. We are much more inclined to make decisions that are in line with a greater purpose. By having a clear vision, the small adjustments, like steering a car, become automatic. Naturally and easily, we correct our course towards our ultimate goals without even thinking about it. We are much less likely to make a decision that has negative consequences, because we are crystal clear on our destination. By understanding our destination and our purpose, we easily attract situations and opportunities into our life that are in line with this purpose. We build our internal and external resources that enable us to enjoy an upward spiral of success.

The internal resources include our subconscious mind, our intuition, our gut feelings, our conscious decision-making ability, signature strengths, etc. The external resources include our relationships, time, money, skills, physical environment, community, and more. These resources are built up using many of the techniques outlined in this book. They include positivity, meditation, mindfulness, gratitude, exercise, identifying strengths, building relationships and, of course, knowledge. When we incorporate these resources into our fundamental foundation of success, we are able to transform our lives to one full of meaning, purpose, and accomplishment.

# Chapter 2

## *Why*

*"There are two great days in a person's life - the day
we are born and the day we discover why"*
*William Barclay*

In order to make any changes in our life, we need a solid "why". Why do we want or need to make the change in the first place? Our why is what creates our emotions. Emotion originally came from the word motion, or "to set in motion". It is our emotion that drives our motivation. The more we can build a solid and meaningful "why", why we need to make changes in our life, why we need to succeed, why we need to change, the stronger our emotions are around that change. The stronger our emotions are, the more motion or motivation we have.

As we build our motivation and begin to engage actively in our world, we develop a sense of joy, happiness, and well-being. This in turn drives us towards happiness and success. My "why" began with my young family and beginning to understand the real cost of working long hours. Running projects over weekends, always on the phone or on site, meant loosing valuable time with my young kids. Eventually, I began to understand the time I was losing with the kids was worth more than the high wage. Once I understood this, I begun a transition to my coaching, where I did not have the same after hour's commitments, so it became easier to enjoy time with my family.

Happiness is not our destination. It is something we enjoy along the way to realizing our dreams, hopes, and aspirations. It's an abstract concept that takes an open mind to understand, a willingness to really grasp the full meaning of and the real benefit to you and your family and friends. We only have one life and with all the challenges and distractions in our modern world, it is virtually impossible, without using the right tools, to step back and appreciate what we have, and to see our opportunities and possibilities.

Our "why" is the reason we need to live a fulfilling and satisfying life. It is the spark, the flame that lights the fire. You will need to develop your own personal and meaningful why. To help you in the process, I would like to outline three main reasons why we must lead happy and fulfilling lives. They are for the kids; our own and/or other children in our lives, our relationships, other people in the community, friends, family, and of course, ourselves. As you read these three reasons, please think about your own personal "why"

## For the Children

Kids are the most compelling reason, for people who have them in their lives. We all want happy children in our lives and we want to be around to enjoy it. When we are always on task, stressed out, and frustrated at home or at work, this is what our children see as normal behaviour. How happy or unhappy you are dramatically effects how happy and successful your kids, or other kids who look up to you, become. Imagine what my kids used to think when I was on the phone over the weekends and even sometimes on holidays? Is this really the example I wanted to give them?

Albert Schweitzer, born in 1875, was a philosopher and physician, among other things; he looked after children. He said something that is still relevant today. *"There are only three ways to teach a child. The first is by example, the second is by example, and the third is by example."* How much better is it for the children in our lives to see us enjoying sport, engaged in our hobbies, and passionate about our interests?

My wife Cathy loves her running. She does all crazy stuff like half marathons and the Tough Mudder events. When I take the kids to cheer her on, I can almost hear their brains processing the fact that Cathy is not just a mum, she has a life just like other people! They realize that exercise and taking on challenges are normal parts of life. I love my music, play a bit of guitar and am in the local choir. After the kids have come to listen to me sing, the house is full of music for weeks.

In coaching and training, there is a popular saying, "What you focus on expands." We will explore this concept later in the book. When we focus on a hobbies or interests, they naturally expand and flow to all areas of our life, including our home, work, and personal life. This goes for the interest itself, and also the feelings and attitudes that accompany it, whether it is sporty, studious, musical, or artistic. They all become part of our life. The kids get involved and become genuinely interested in what we are doing.

How often does the child of a passionate football player become a football player, or a child of a musician become interested in music? The same goes for negativity. We all know of poorly behaved kids who come from families that are just not functioning as well as they could. Attitudes like passion or calmness are infectious, unfortunately so is laziness or stress. So the best way to teach our kids how to enjoy a fulfilling and happy life is to enjoy a fulfilling and happy life ourselves.

## Relationships

Of course life is not just about the kids. It is about our relationships; our partners, friends, and extended family, and others in our community. If you are in a relationship, you may think that spending more time looking after yourself may not be fair to your partner. Do you feel guilty? Is it fair? Remember, they fell in love with us (usually) before kids, or before all the other hassles in life came along. We were not mum's and dad's, workers or managers, we were people! We enjoyed life! We had sports, hobbies and interests.

If you are looking for that someone special, there is no better way to make this happen than to enjoy life, your sports, hobbies, and interests. By challenging ourselves and getting out of our comfort zone, we open ourselves to new opportunities. We meet new people and enjoy more social interaction in healthy and happy environments.

Have you ever challenged yourself, put yourself out of your comfort zone, in a sport, hobby, or other interest only to find you really enjoyed it? It was fun right? You may have been nervous or even skeptical at first, but it all worked out in the end. Now think, did doing this deepen your relationship with another person? Did you meet someone new? Living happy and fulfilling lives helps build our relationship with our partners, children, family, friends, and other people in our community. This in turn makes us happy!

David Whyte the poet calls this the "Third Marriage". In his book "Three Marriages: Reimagining Work, Self & Relationship" he explores this... our first marriage to our partner, the second to our vocation, and the third to ourselves.

## Ourselves

It is critical for our own well-being, our health, and happiness, to take time out regularly to do something for ourselves. Think for a moment, if you had a little more time energy and even money, what would you love to do? Or do more of? It could be as simple as playing tennis with friends once a week, riding your bike, or going surfing. It could be more ambitious, like writing a book, traveling, or climbing Mount Everest.

What are your sports, hobbies, or interests? Think about it, are you still doing them, are you still living life? Or have you, like many of us with all the pressures of work and family, slipped back into your comfort zone? Here we can live a good life, but will not always be getting the very most out of life, not always thriving or finding meaning and purpose in what we do.

Is there anything you love doing that you are not enjoying now? Do you have anything that you would like to do more of? Our own happiness and success is so important to our family, our friends and most importantly, ourselves. It is so important we need to find the energy and motivation to get out and enjoy a happy, meaningful, and fulfilling life. It is so important that would be crazy not to take a well thought out and focussed course of action, to ensure that we are empowered to accomplish our dreams and desires.

# Chapter 3

## Four Steps to Change

*"Sometimes if you want to see a change for the better,
you have to take things into your own hands"*
*Clint Eastwood*

To succeed in work or in life, we should use all the relevant tools and techniques available to us. The real trick is to review all of these techniques and decide which ones resonate best with you. Everyone is different; so much care should be taken to choose the right path. Some people are extremely confident, so need little help with self-esteem. Some people are extremely social, so do not need to work on their social relationships.

In order to really succeed, you should be aware of your weaknesses but focus on your strengths. In this book, I will discuss many concepts and techniques that can be used to achieve success easily and naturally. Whichever tools and techniques you decide to utilize, to achieve what you most want in work and life, you should have a solid foundation from which you can integrate your own ideas, the various techniques in this book, and ones from other sources.

As a coach, I have studied successful people from all around the world and from all types of disciplines; sports people wanting to win the gold medal, or a championship, a CEO looking to increase profits, workers looking to maximize their income by way of promotion or career change, or a parent trying to build a successful family unit. They all use a common and effective foundation.

The foundation can be summarized in four stages
1. Have a clear dream or vision of what you want to achieve
2. Set specific goals in order to achieve the dream
3. Prepare plans for each goal
4. Take action

For simplicity, this book will review each of the four steps above. They are easy to understand and implement in your life. From a more scientific perspective, Richard Boyatzis from Case Western Reserve University, Cleveland, Ohio, USA, has studied this process in depth. It is a more complex system and is called the Intentional Change Theory (ICT), which is motivated by the discovery of the "Ideal Self." His research paper describes it as follows --"The change process actually involves a sequence of discontinuities, called discoveries, which function as an iterative cycle in producing the sustainable change at the individual level. These are:

(1) *The ideal self and a personal vision;*

(2) *The real self and its comparison to the ideal self, resulting in an assessment of one's strengths and weaknesses, in a sense a personal balance sheet;*

(3) *A learning agenda and plan;*

(4) *Experimentation and practice with the new behavior, thoughts, feelings, or perceptions; and*

(5) *Trusting, or resonant relationships that enable a person to experience and process each discovery in the process."*

Richard E. Boyatzis. An overview of intentional change from a complexity perspective, Case Western Reserve University, Cleveland, Ohio, USA

Think of an Olympic athlete. They dream to stand on the top of the dais, with their national anthem playing while the world watches. They dream to be the fastest and/or best in their field. They have very specific goals around what competitions they need to compete in and the level they need to achieve to make the Olympic team. They have goals around their training, their diet, and their dedication. They have well-prepared plans for each goal. Last but not least they take massive action.

A CEO dreams of leading their company to success. They have goals relating to their financial targets, expenditure, and new products or services that make them stand out from their competitor. They create detailed plans to achieve each goal and are always taking action.

Successful workers dream of the pay rise, promotion, or new opportunity. They set goals towards their advancements and prepare plans around those goals. Every day, they take action towards creating a better future for themselves and their businesses. Even parents, especially the more successful ones, have dreams of how their family life should be. They dream of the holidays, their home, and their children succeeding at school. They set goals, prepare plans, and take action.

There is true power in having a solid structure on which to build your success. By having a solid structure, you will find clarity, direction, and motivation, which will drive you along your journey to your perfect life. A solid foundation in your work and your personal life allows you to better utilize your strengths and passions across both domains. It is the structure that makes it easier to prioritize your efforts and to understand where your focus will provide you with the most rewards. It will allow you to navigate the complex web of life and to bring knowledge and power from one domain to the other.

We have infinitely more power to change, improve, and decide the direction of our lives than we could ever imagine. The good news is we can access this power by following these four simple steps. A process of change that is easy, effective, and extremely powerful.

Life is mysterious and intangible. We don't just live in the physical plane; there are at least the mental, emotional, and spiritual planes as well. Results cannot always be explained, nor can you predict all the outcomes that may occur when you decide to take control of your life.

The outer world is a reflection of our inner world. When we take the time to develop our inner self, we will discover limitless possibilities and experience a thriving transformation.

> *"On this path, it is only the first step that counts."*
> *St Jean- Baptiste-Marie Vianney, Catholic Saint, Cure' d'Ars*

The power of the four steps comes in their simplicity. Great things will happen that you did not see coming; things you never could have planned for; people, experiences, and new possibilities. The power of the steps comes from the gifts you receive along the way. The intangible nature of our very existence means that things are not always as they seem, rewards are not always equal to the effort, and that meaningful transformations can be made with small changes in our direction and perspective.

> *"Until one is committed, there is hesitancy, the chance to draw back,*
> *ineffectiveness. Concerning all acts of initiative (and creation), there*
> *is one elementary truth, the ignorance that kills countless ideas and*
> *splendid truth: that moment where one defiantly commits oneself, then*
> *provenance moves too. A whole stream of events issues from the decision,*
> *raising in favor all manner of unforeseen incidents, meetings and material*
> *assistance, which no man could have dreamed would have come his way."*
> *W.H Murray, Explorer*

# Chapter 4

## The Dream

*"If you can dream it, you can do it"*
*Walt Disney*

The first step towards happiness and success is to dream. You need a crystal clear vision of your perfect life. Think for a moment of what drives you, what motivates you; think of the happiest you have ever been, the most excited. When you were full of energy, think of where you were and what you were doing. Use this as inspiration, as a signpost toward what you really want to be doing with your life.

The dream or vision is not what other people want you to be or do; it's the real you, what you really want to accomplish. Be selfish and be bold. You should write it out or use a vision board. If you write it, write it as though it is already happening, like you are there. Get creative and put in as much detail as you can. Go for excitement; it is not all about happiness and being comfortable. Let loose and really use your imagination.

Some people love using the vision board. A vision board is where you create a board, as big or small as you like. On it, you put inspirational pictures, quotes, and/or words that reflect your vision, your dream. The idea is to stir up as many emotions around your goals as you can. For example, if you always wanted to play tennis competitively, you may have a picture of the center court in Wimbledon, or a picture of a tennis player up on the dais. If your dream is to play social tennis, it may be a picture of a tennis racket or people having drinks next to the court at a local tennis club. You build a collage of inspirational pictures and words that reflect your dream, your vision of all you want out of life.

When deciding what to put on your vision board, or in your written vision statement, please make sure that the vision is yours. Try to avoid having a vision that has been artificially put on you, for example, through advertising, mass media, friend or family. Your vision should be true to you.

It has been shown through research, called the Perceived Locus of Causality Model, by Richard M. Ryan and James P. Connell, of the University of Rocheste, there is a difference of motivation between when we do things we are told to do, things we feel we should do, thinks we like doing and things we LOVE doing!.

A person's motivation changes greatly when they want to or choose to do something, as compared to if they are acting from guilt or obligation, that is, when they feel they should or must behave in a given way. These are self-concordant goals. Self-concordance refers to the degree to which a goal is aligned with an individual's intrinsic interests, motivations and values. Ideally your dream should reflect what you really want to do, what you love doing. Of course there may be some compromise required here, yet if you can at least want to achieve your dream, for your own personal reasons, rather than feeling you need to achieve them for external reasons, you will have a much better chance of success.

> *"Your time is limited, so don't waste it living someone else's life.*
> *Don't be trapped by dogma — which is living with the results of*
> *other people's thinking. Don't let the noise of others' opinions drown*
> *out your own inner voice. And most important, have the courage*
> *to follow your heart and intuition. They somehow already know*
> *what you truly want to become. Everything else is secondary"*
> *Steve Jobs - Commencement speech at Stanford University in 2005*

It has also been shown, that you are much more likely to achieve your vision if you have at least 70% chance of achieving it. After all, positive thinking is great; yet however powerful your vision is, you must also believe that you can accomplish it. Sometimes a vision or dream should be broken down into smaller components so they become more achievable. They should be achievable and true to you.

They can be challenging; in fact research tells us we are more likely to achieve more challenging goals. But if they become too outside the realm of possible accomplishment, then they may work against you. Take, for example, the dream of winning Wimbledon. If you are already on the professional circuit, a picture of Center Court at Wimbledon may be appropriate on your vision board. If you are only in a local competition, you may be best served with a picture of a regional or national competition. This does not mean you cannot include Wimbledon as well, nor does this exclude the ability to change the picture/vision from a national competition to Wimbledon once you achieve the goal of the national competition.

I always dreamed of being able to sing and play guitar. I could see myself up on stage and playing my songs to an appreciative audience. It has always been lower on the list of priorities, than owning my home, getting married, having kids and traveling. Yet as time went on. I have kept playing and writing songs. I have played in front of audiences, although not often and even started a band with a few friends. I have recorded a CD and still love to play. The best thing about this dream for me, is that it gives me something still to strive for. Something to developed and work on. It is a passion that has enhanced my life in ways that is hard to explain. It is a passion that I want only for myself. If I stop playing, no other person in the whole world will really care. This has given it real power personally, as I can really enjoy the small progress I make, knowing that I am not letting anyone down.

Goals do not always need to be change the world type stuff. We can use them to help us with less life changing interests. You may just want to learn to play piano, learn to paint, go surfing or, do talk back at the local radio station. The more personal they are to you, they more enjoyment and also motivation you get from them.

When I encourage clients to write a vision of their ideal world, their perfect life, I try to establish some reality behind the dream or goal. So when you envisage your ideal life, you should remove self-limiting doubts and negative thoughts (we will deal with these separately later) and always keep in mind the possibility of success. Dreams and visions, by their very nature, should be updated and reviewed regularly. As you achieve some short-term dreams, or become more confident and further along in your journey, you may change the dream.

It may sound like a fine line between not dwelling on the negatives and being unrealistic in your expectations. Please keep in mind that negative thoughts and emotions generally have more power than the positive ones.

So for the sake of exploring what is possible, please remember that no one is holding you to this; it is your dream, your vision, so really let loose.

The best thing you can do to enjoy life is to challenge yourself, to grow, and to help others. Envision what you're perfect life would be, where would you work, where would you live, what you would do for fun and fulfillment, who your friends would be, what you would eat, what sports would you play, and how you get your exercise on a day-to-day basis. The idea of the dream or vision is to keep it broad. This keeps your options open. You are trying to capture the feelings and emotions, and the type of sports, or other activities you desire most. You do not need to decide the exact club, or where or how you will fulfill your dream. Put it all on paper, either written down or as a vision board. This is the key.

It is as important, maybe more, to dream about what you need to remove from your life than what you need to add to your life. We call it removing roadblocks. They could be bad relationships, unfulfilling careers, laziness, or addictions. I'm talking about drinking, smoking, gambling, excess sugar, caffeine, fatty foods, or a poor diet. Roadblocks could include your self-limiting beliefs ("I'm not good enough to do this or that," "I am not smart enough," and the list goes on).

It has been proven time and time and again that removing roadblocks brings you clarity, motivation, confidence, and builds up your self-esteem. Removing the roadblocks energizes you, so achieving your goals becomes easy and natural and, as a result, you find success and abundance.

We all know our roadblocks; we often say that we will fix them tomorrow, but now is the time. So when you write down your dream, forget the things in your life that you don't want. Write down your dream without these things, including how you will feel without them, how much more time, energy, or money you will have without them. This is how we unleash the power within. Removing the roadblocks then becomes easy.

We want the dream to be as detailed and crystal clear as possible. What we're trying to capture is the direction of your beliefs and values. It should be a vision of the sort of life you want, including your health and your lifestyle. As you continue along the journey, your dream may change as you discover expanding possibilities. We don't want to get locked into a rigid vision, or limit our options. It will set you up for disappointment if things do not turn out exactly as you planned.

What we need to change, aside from our behavior, are our pervasive thoughts, feelings, and emotions. So, when you write down your dream, it is essential to write how you feel, think, behave, and notice what your emotional state is. Are you happy, enthusiastic, keen, or excited? "I have been so happy since I changed jobs; the people are great and I love the challenge." The more you can capture these emotional states, the easier the change is. It is your environment and situation that supports these feelings and thoughts and all these things together drive change.

Once you are clear on your dream, discover and decide the goals required to achieve your dream. It can be useful to use a separate page for each category. You can decide on your own or you can start with the basics; career, relationships, financial, health, spiritual and physical well-being. Goals allow us to see the individual step in the process. They allow us to focus on each task individually and have a sense of satisfaction when we accomplish it.

Ultimately, we want our dreams and visions to be broad and we want our goals to be specific. We want to do this with checkpoints along the way to celebrate our successes and for a chance to review our progress, receive feedback, and re-evaluate to ensure we are on track and are taking advantage of any new possibilities that may have arisen.

## Businesses use vision statements

Businesses use short vision statements. They then elaborate on those short vision statements with more detailed statements and also a mission statement. These vision statements can have a major effect on the way a business operates, and can determine its ultimate success or failure. Sometimes when we look at the vision statement, it is all too easy to think its some fluffy terminology that's designed to look good nicely framed in the foyer. We sometimes think the vision statement has nothing to do with the day-to-day operation of the business. This is wrong.

About 30 years ago, Microsoft had a simple vision statement; Put a computer on every desktop and in every home. This was in the very early days of computing and the internet. We see now how that early vision from Bill Gates manifested itself. Around the same time, 20 years before iPads, iPhones, and iPods, Apple Computers, as it was known then, had a different vision statement. Their vision was; A computer in the hands of everyday people. What we can clearly see from this example is that Microsoft was focusing on people sitting at desks using their product. They were also focused on, and achieved, a mass roll out and uptake. Apple, on the other hand, had a vision of ease-of-use (for everyday people) and portability (in the hands of). In this example, we can clearly see the power of a vision.

I will share a few others with you to drive home the point. Disney: To make people happy. Instagram; To capture and share the world's moments. Google; To access the world's information in one click.

Just imagine the power of a clear, concise, and well thought-out vision in your business, life, sporting group, or club! We too often think of a vision statement as a corporate tool, however, they are just as powerful a tool for our own happiness and success. That said, we are a lot less likely to use a vision statement in our own lives. I strongly recommend that everyone has a clear vision. This can start with one line as they do in business.

When we use them personally, however, elaborating on our vision with the written word or on a vision board gives it so much more meaning because it is directed to you by you. You should aim to give it as much emotion and passion as possible. Remember, the whole idea of documenting your vision is not just to tell your conscious mind what you want. It is to allow your subconscious mind and all your automatic responses to work towards this vision. Our subconscious mind works less directly than our conscious mind. It communicates with our consciousness and the external world through thoughts, feelings, and emotions. Therefore, the more passion we can conjure up when creating our vision statement or vision board, the more passion, feelings, and emotions this vision invokes in us when we see it or read it.

Having a clear vision, builds on the passion and emotion we used to create it. It lets us feel it, touch it and see it. We are better able to find the meaning in our vision, and understand why it is so important to us, we can then find meaning. We can find motivation, success, and accomplishment. We are clear on our direction so we will not be swayed by external forces. When we are clear on our vision, we decide the life that we live. By deciding the direction and focus of our own lives, we have a greater chance to find fulfillment and meaning. Everything we do starts to align with what we really want out of life, which obviously gives us a greater chance of achieving it. It also minimizes sidetracks, distractions, anxiety, and confusion. Even more so than helping us with our day to day life, it helps us understand the big picture.

Once we know the big picture, what we want from life, we are a lot less likely to let years go by unaccounted for. From a major life regret perspective, a clear vision becomes our best friend. No one wants to wake up one morning in midlife and wonder what happened. No one wants to wake up and feel regret for wasted years. No one should leave the game of life to chance. We have enough challenges and roadblocks in life already. By having a clear direction, a clear vision of what we want out of life, we are in control, and in a much better position to get back on track when the inevitable challenges of life fall upon us.

# Chapter 5

# Creating Success with Goals

*"Success is steady progress toward one's personal goals"*
*Jim Rohn*

Why is there always so much to do? So many things in our lives that we need to achieve and so little time. Don't you find that the days, weeks, months, and even years just fly by? There is always much more that needs to be done. The last thing I want to do is to add anything more to my list!

I used to think if I just worked hard, try my best, it would all turn out okay. It usually does and life keeps going. We still get up in the morning and eat breakfast, do our work for the day, try to relax in the evening, and have a good sleep. So why add another level of complexity? Why should I even think about adding goals to my list of things to do? There are so many people in my life telling me what to do, why should I start telling myself what to do too?

Goals, it turns out, actually make our life a lot easier. As we will see in this section, by having clear and sometimes challenging goals, our actions become more efficient and effective. There is less wasted time, less confusion, and less frustration. We put oil in our engine, grease on the chain or on the wheels. It smoothes out the ride, it removes friction, it makes our cars, our bikes and billy carts flow freely. The same is true with goals and our lives. By adding something, in this case our goals not oil, we are actually smoothing the ride. We are increasing our speed and efficiency; we are greasing the wheels of life.

I cannot overstate the importance of focus. What else is a goal really, than focus? When we focus in on a task, it flows. Think of when you play billiards, tennis, play music, or doing anything that you truly love. Don't you find that you do your best when you focus? When you focus on what you love, or what is important, and forget external distractions, you get into the flow. Nothing else matters, but the current task at hand. You become one with the challenge of the task. This is when you achieve success. This is when you play your best music, win billiards, or tennis. When you are focused and in the flow, everything becomes easy. When you are focused and in the flow, you perform at your best. Like the oil in a car, or the grease on a chain, you are moving quickly and efficiently with minimal resistance. You are achieving the most with the least effort.

Now I want you to think about one of your big challenges. It may be at work, study, or from your sports, hobbies, and interests. Now ask yourself; how often do you fully focus on the challenge? How often do you give it 100% attention? Take your career, as an example, because becoming successful in our work, our careers, is one of the best ways to set ourselves up for life. It builds our self-confidence, our sense of meaning, and of course, brings financial security. Our work is so important, yet many people fail to set specific, challenging, achievable goals within the workplace. These goals can, and should be, both day-to-day goals and long-term goals.

How often do you focus on your work without allowing for any other distractions? These distractions could include personal texts, phone, or email. They may be work-related distractions, such as checking email to often, performing tasks that are not in line with your prime purpose, returning phone calls and emails that someone else has put a priority on, etc. By setting clear and concise goals in the workplace, we are able to achieve much more on any given day. By having clear and specific longer term goals, we are able to restructure, and re-craft our work environment to lean towards building our skills, contacts, and other resources to achieve our longer term goal. This passion to set and achieve goals is even less common in individual's personal lives. By having career and personal goals, we are in a far better chance to have a fulfilling, meaningful, and successful life than we could possibly dream of without them.

Far too many people spend more time planning their weekends more than their lives. Then they wonder why they get the feeling life has passed them by without knowing what happened. When you are clear on your goals, what you really most desire in life, you begin to focus your mind and concentrate your energy on what you wish to achieve. One of the great advantages of having a definite goal for your life is that it helps you prioritize your activities. When you are very clear in your mind on what you want to achieve, it is unnecessary to analyze each individual situation. You know automatically whether your actions will move you toward your goal or away from it. You can then use all of your resources, time, money, and energy to the best advantage.

In 1996, Edwin Locke at the University of Maryland conducted a 30-year study into the relationship between goal setting and performance. It included tens of thousands of people. It found that the more difficult and specific the goal, the greater the achievement. It also found that if the individual believed the goal was important and achievable and used feedback to show progress, there was a greater level of success. These studies showed that "Specific, high (hard) goals lead to a higher level of task performance than do easy goals or vague, abstract goals such as the exhortation to ``do one's best."

So long as a person is committed to the goal, has the requisite ability to attain it, and does not have conflicting goals, there is a positive, linear relationship between goal difficulty and task. Goals are related to affect in that goals set the primary standard for self-satisfaction with performance. High, or hard, goals are motivating because they require one to attain more in order to be satisfied than do low, or easy, goals. Feelings of success in the workplace occur to the extent that people see that they are able to grow and meet job challenges by pursuing and attaining goals that are important and meaningful.[1]"

More challenging goals lead to greater effort and/or persistence than do moderately difficult, easy, or vague goals. Goals direct attention, focus, effort, and drives toward goal-relevant actions at the expense of non-relevant actions. They also allow us to focus on the task. It gives that task meaning, because we know how it will help us achieve our dream or vision. We can put the goal into context against the bigger picture of life.

By understanding our goals, we are in a better position to know exactly what we need to learn and discover all the resources required to achieve that goal. These goals provide us with motivation, as suggested in Locke's goal setting theory "Goals may simply motivate one to use one's existing ability, may automatically 'pull' stored task relevant knowledge into awareness, and/or may motivate people to search for new knowledge.

The latter is most common when people are confronted by new, complex tasks.[2]"

Sometimes it is effective to set goals around what knowledge we need to attain to achieve a larger goal or dream. For example, one study[3] found that "Entering MBA students who set specific difficult learning goals (e.g., learn to network, master specific course subject matter) subsequently had higher GPAs and higher satisfaction with their MBA program than did people who simply set a distal (long-term or end) performance goal for GPA at the end of the academic year. By having goals around what the students need to learn, that helped them with their planning and monitoring progress."

In this chapter we have looked at approach goals, the ones we aim for and strive for. The opposite are avoidance goals. These goals are not as effective. Diets usually fail because people set avoidance goals.

If we keep telling ourselves not to do this or that, we tend to think about those things we want to avoid. These things become on our mind constantly and we can never move away from them. This is why I suggest approach goals. We move forward toward what we want, rather than away from what we do not want. We focus on the solution not the problem.

# Chapter 6

# Goal setting and motivation in the work place

*"The productivity of a work group seems to depend on how the group members see their own goals in relation to the goals of the organization"*
*Ken Blanchard*

Goals have been extensively used in business to achieve results. Most organizations have some form of goal setting strategy. Programs such as key performance indicators, high-performance work practices, benchmarking, sales targets, as well as strategic planning all include the development of specific goals. I have seen some of these techniques used very well and some very poorly. Ultimately, the times that I have seen goal setting or targets at work bring success is when the goal is challenging, and when the individual achieves it, they are recognised and appreciated. Goal setting is the underlying explanation for all major theories of work motivation, whether that be Maslow's work on motivation and personality, Herzberg's motivation theories or others. Managers widely accept goal setting as a means to improve and sustain performance.

Based on hundreds of studies, the major finding of goal setting is that individuals who are provided with specific, difficult but attainable goals, perform better than those given easy, non-specific goals, or no goals at all. At the same time, the individuals must have sufficient ability, accept the goals, and receive feedback related to performance. Goals need to be accepted. Simply assigning goals to organization members may not result in their commitment to those goals, especially if the goal will be difficult to accomplish. "A powerful method of obtaining acceptance is to allow organization members to participate in the goal-setting process. In other words, participation in the goal-setting process tends to enhance goal commitment. Participation helps organization members better understand the goals, ensure that the goals are not unreasonable, and helps them achieve the goal."[4]

All of this overflow from one domain to another and how well it works for you, relies on two things; self-regulation and using goals to monitor performance. By monitoring our performance against specific goals we are able to change what's not working, and do more of what works. We modify our plans accordingly. We can regulate our behavior to maximise our success.

In this complex world of interdependence, it is often difficult to achieve our goals without help from others. This is true in the business world and our personal lives. How often have you been on track to achieve your goals only to be let down by someone else? The obvious answer to this problem is to include the other person in your goals; to build up a shared vision of what you need to achieve together. The more other people who share our goals in our work and personal life, the more chance we have to succeed. It is often not the immediate task at hand that is the most important, but the big picture. When we all share the same vision, or big picture, especially in large organizations, we have the greatest chance to succeed.

## Shared Goals

Shared goals and visions are especially important in big teams and organizations. The more diverse the people and teams involved, the more important it is that they connect through a shared vision and goals. A study of companies and their suppliers in China found that "The relationship between a high level of a shared vision among employees and low levels of dysfunctional opportunism was partially mediated by the setting of cooperative goals. A shared vision strengthened cooperative goal setting by drawing the boundary lines of the group around the two organizations involved--namely, the company and its suppliers--thereby reducing the negative feelings that frequently occur in alliances due to perceptions of in- versus out-groups."[5]

A study in 2004[6] designed to uncover the performance of small-venture entrepreneurs over a 6-year period found "Goals around growth and a vision for the future, was found to significantly predict future growth. Once a goal is accepted and understood, it becomes a reference point for guiding and giving meaning to subsequent mental and physical actions."

## Goal setting for teams

The key to success in goal setting in teams is that individual goals should be in line with the team goals. One study involving 324 members of 64 short-term project teams explored how bringing together personal, team, and performance goals affected individual outcomes. Results indicated that "Bringing together performance goals elicited greater individual satisfaction and contributions, regardless of how simple or difficult the goal was."[7] Think of a time you played sport as a team. Did you not try harder because the team depended on it?

## Productivity and Cost Improvement

Numerous studies have shown that "Setting a specific difficult goal leads to significant increases in employee productivity."[8] Think back to a time in your own work life where the team was extremely productive. Was everyone clear on what the team was trying to achieve? Was your own personal challenge, or goal, directly related to the team's goal? In a study on loggers, "Loggers cut more trees,"[9] and "unionized truck drivers increased the logs loaded on their trucks from 60% to 90% of the legal allowable weight as a result of assigned goals. The drivers saved the company $250,000 in 9 months."[10] In an office-based study "Word-processing operators with specific high goals increased their performance regardless of whether the goal was assigned or set participatively."[11] In a survey of companies from Dun's Business Rankings, they found "A significant correlation between goal setting and organizational profitability."[12] Productivity in our own workplace is not only good for our employer, it is good for us. We are more satisfied with work because it is going well. Research shows how this work satisfaction flows into our personnel life. We all know how good we feel when work is going well, and conversely, how hard it is to be excited about life when work is getting us down.

# Feedback

Feedback is very important in the process of achieving goals. Firstly, it helps by letting us know how we are doing. As we make progress towards our goals, we are motivated to keep going. The closer we get, the more motivation we have. Like a marathon runner starts to speed up near the end of the race, we get an extra shot of energy, knowing we are getting closer to our goal. We gain satisfaction as we make progress. This is especially true when we are receiving feedback from of peers, friends, and co-workers. This makes us feel valued and our progress has more meaning, because we are sharing our progress with others. Secondly, feedback allows us to adjust our methods and strategies as it is often hard to self-evaluate.

By receiving feedback from others, providing we are open to their suggestions, we may find a faster, more efficient or better way of completing the task. The feedback gives us critical insight into what we are doing. Even when we do not adopt the suggestions or recommendations from others, it allows us to view the task from alternate perspectives. This alternate perspective is often all we need to make the breakthrough that is required.

Feedback could also come from a video or recording of what we are doing. This technique is often used by sports coaches, music teachers, directors of plays, and such. Reviewing the visual or audio feedback of our efforts, especially in addition to a coach's or mentor's perspective or recommendations, we have a powerful tool to help us improve our performance.

Even on more personal goals, feedback is critical. Whether your goal is around diet, exercise, career change or advancement, financial, or in any other domain of your life, finding the right tool for the feedback is critical. You may use a coach, trainer, adviser, or just a friend or family member. The important thing in any goal is to understand that feedback is an extremely valuable tool and should be actively sought after. We are accustomed to taking on many of our life challenges on our own.

Sometimes we are ashamed to ask, sometimes we just don't think anyone can help. You will find when you actively seek feedback that people are much more ready to supply it than you might imagine. I challenge you to undertake a simple experiment. Next time you are in the process of chasing a specific goal, actively seek someone who can give you feedback. Take note of whether the feedback is useful or not. Even if you feel the specific feedback received was not useful, did it not provide you with another perspective? By keeping an open mind and actively looking for feedback in anything we undertake, we are giving ourselves a better opportunity for success.

## Goals as a tool to Evaluate Performance

We are more successful in a task when it can be measured. If we are dieting and we have a goal to lose 10 kg, we will achieve that goal easier and faster if we make a habit of weighing ourselves and tracking our progress. This is so obvious that not many people would think of trying to achieve weight loss without monitoring progress. If our goal is sports related, such as swimming, and we have a goal of achieving a specific time for the 100 m or such, we track our progress, and monitor how close we get to our goal. We also know that as we get closer to our set time, we put in that extra bit of effort.

In the work environment, sales people are well-known to have monthly targets. Call center operators have goals around average speed of answer, abandonment rates, issue completion, etc. CEOs have goals around profitability, project managers have goals around completion times and expenditure, and customer service representatives have goals around customer satisfaction.

Using goals to boost performance at work is common practice. It is effective because we know what we need to achieve, when we need to achieve it, and how it is measured. These goals give us direction and purpose. They give us meaning and a sense of purpose, which is magnified when it is a shared team effort or common goal. The key in this situation is that we can measure progress. By measuring progress, not only are we able to compensate and reward people who achieve their goals, but we can understand clearly our own performance. Like feedback, this understanding allows us to adjust our strategies, commitment, or any other method used to achieve these goals.

So why are we often resistant to setting goals in our own lives? Setting our own personal work goals, relationship goals, or any number of goals within our own personal life allows us to measure and evaluate our performance. By doing so, we are in a much better position to change or adjust what we are doing to ensure maximum performance.

Maximizing performance is not just running faster. It may mean losing more weight, becoming fitter, more financially secure, have better relationships, or just to feel happier. Not only are goal setting techniques from the workplace useful in our everyday life, but by using them in our lives, we are getting better at setting and achieving goals. The better we become at setting and achieving our goals, the better our life is overall. A client of mine recently said he needed to decide where his focus should be; should he focus on his career or his social life. The answer of course should be obvious; everything is interconnected.

By becoming more successful in our career, we build up our network of friends and colleagues, our social skills, our disposable income (we hope), our confidence, and general life satisfaction. By building up our social life, we build our critical social skills, our confidence, our well-being and life satisfaction. By using goals to build our performance in one life domain, this increased performance naturally overflows to other domains. Many studies, including ones mentioned in his book, show a strong correlation between life satisfaction and work satisfaction and vice versa.

# Chapter 7

## *Goals in our personal life*

*"What you get by achieving your goals is not as important*
*as what you become by achieving your goals"*
*Zig Ziglar and Henry David Thoreau*

Just as succeeding in work helps us at home, succeeding at home helps us at work. Goals at work are common practice, not so much in our personal life. For this reason, when setting personal goals, we should take active steps to make sure they are meaningful for us. Share your goals with friends and family; give your program a name or even make a logo. The more you personally buy into your own program of action, the greater the chance of success. The goal itself is the direction. It is important to understand the difference between a vision and a goal and to complete all four steps to change; the dream or vision, goals, planning, and action. There is abundant research that proves that this simple process is effective and can bring on real meaningful and inspirational changes in our lives.

## Solution-focused goals

It is easier to move toward your goals than away from your old habits. Do not dwell in the past, move toward, not away. Coaching (yourself or using a coach) is future orientated. Goals are not about repairing the past as much as they are about creating the future. Always move towards solutions and not away from problems. The problem is something you have; the problems are not you. Forget the problem and work on the solution. Be solution-focused; it's proven to work better. If you need help on your journey, be sure to find some help. It could be a friend or family member, a co-worker or a coach. Think about it. Don't you feel so much better striving and achieving something you are interested in, rather than dealing with life's issues?

> *"Everyone needs a coach. It doesn't matter whether you're a*
> *basketball player, a tennis player, a gymnast or a bridge player"*
> *Bill Gates, Microsoft*

## Types of goal setting

Personal goal setting is "A self-regulatory process that affects an individual's behaviors and actions, often in ways we did not plan, nor could not predict. Also, the type of goals we strive for have an impact on how successful we are. The type of goal an individual strives for also influences his well-being in several ways."[13] For instance, studies show "People who are engaged in interpersonal goals (e.g. doing voluntary work at the community center) tend to report higher subjective well-being than people who are engaged in intra-personal or more self-oriented goals (e.g. jogging every night)." The way we feel about our goals also matters. Research shows "People who are committed to personal endeavors that are manageable, meaningful and supported, generally report higher well-being than people who are engaged in goals that do not have these characteristics."[14] Furthermore, according to Self-Determination Theory,[15] "Autonomous goals (e.g., striving for personal growth or enjoyment) are inherently rewarding because they satisfy innate psychological needs such as relatedness, competence and autonomy."

It is important our goals, where possible, are self-motivated. That is, that we want these things for their own sake and understand they will help us. Self-determination theory tells us "When people are autonomously motivated, they experience volition, or a self-endorsement of their actions. In contrast, controlled goals (e.g., those that are pursued to please someone else or to gain fame) do not directly satisfy these psychological needs to the same extent; people tend to experience pressure to think, feel, or behave in particular ways."[16] This concept was explained very well in an article called Goals, Congruence, and Positive Well-being; "Several longitudinal studies have shown that the pursuit of autonomous goals is positively related to various well-being indicators whereas the pursuit of controlled goals is negatively related to these indicators.[17] Simply put, well-being levels improve when individuals are autonomous and feel they have the power of choice when pursuing their goals. This well-being is enhanced even more if the goal is meaningful and personal.

As I am writing this book, I am extremely motivated. It is something I am passionate about and I want to do. No one is forcing me to write it. I believe it is for this reason, I am happy to spend hours adding and editing it, without even thinking about doing some other pleasure-seeking activity.

## Small goals add up

Goals should be challenging yet achievable. We know that we should have a 70% chance of succeeding. Another dimension that relates to goal success is how far away the end is. Consider as an example that you want to run a full marathon. You don't run much at all at the moment, but the thought of running a full marathon really excites you. Your vision, your dream, and goal is to run through the finishing line of the Boston Marathon, Sydney City to Surf, or a local marathon. You put a picture of a marathon finishing line on the wall or on your vision board. The next day, you start running. After 3 km, you are exhausted, your legs hurt, and you just want to sit down. You look at the picture of the finishing line and you give up.

Going from 3 km to 42 kilometers is just too big of a jump. Another scenario is that, you investigate some local fun runs, a 5 km, a 10 km and then a half marathon. You cut out pictures and inspirations for all three events. You book in for all three events. A poster on the back of your door, or a small picture on the mantle, shows the finishing line of the Boston Marathon. But the pictures that are more obvious, in constant view, are the entrance confirmations and brochures for the shorter runs. You build support with family and friends, and even enlist some of them to join you. It becomes a talking point with your friends and a mutual interest. Many of them have no intention of running the marathon, but they feel building up to the half marathon would be a worthwhile and challenging goal for them.

You share training plans, meal ideas and plan a little celebration after each event. The whole challenge has become interesting and fun. You build a positive perception and mental attitude towards the ultimate goal of a full marathon. It is not just the ultimate goal that you are now looking forward to but the journey. You run the 5 km, 10 km and ultimately, a half marathon. There is a lot of support and praise from your friends and family. So much so, you have built your confidence and your running ability up to a level where the full marathon seems achievable. You believe that you have over 70% chance of success.

Later that year, you complete the marathon and receive praise and congratulations from a vast amount of family friends and co-workers. By taking on the smaller goals, you kept your motivation going and remained enthusiastic through the process. You built yourself up physically and mentally and were able to accomplish the marathon with more ease than you ever thought. The additional social support that you gained through achieving and celebrating smaller goals in the beginning was essential to achieving the larger goal in the end. This example is equally true for any challenge. It may be a large project at work, or other life goals.

Always take time, to break down larger goals to smaller achievable ones. Ensure you have a high chance of success with the small goals. Make sure you can track progress and celebrate once you achieve them. This will bring tasks or challenges that may have previously seemed unattainable within reach. Remember, the whole idea is to be able to maintain a positive attitude and stay enthusiastic throughout the process.

## Deadlines Improve the Effectiveness of Goals

The completion date or deadline is critical for any goal. Deadline is a funny word, isn't it? We should really call it a success line. In the work environment as the deadline approaches, we have all seen people running around frantically trying to complete the tasks. The deadline increases our motivation and energy and puts a line in the sand for which we are to aim. When we have a target date, or deadline, we become more productive. Parkinson's famous law states that "Work expands so as to fill the time available for its completion."

Deadlines, or success lines, can be equally as effective in our personal life as in our work life. We should also keep in mind that we can set our own success lines, not just always have them as burdens put on us by someone else. Putting timeliness on our own goals is extremely effective and almost mandatory. Imagine if, after an indulgent Christmas holidays, you committed to losing 10kgs. You tell a friend about it, and when they ask by when, you proceed to tell them there is no set time frame. Imagine if you've had a goal of running marathon, but had no time frame of when this should be achieved. Having a clear time frame in which to accomplish the goal is essential. The diet and marathon examples are common, understandable, and very tangible. Where this concept becomes a little tricky is when the goal is a little less tangible or a long way away. Take for example the goal 'I want to be happier' or 'I would like to have more close friends.' Both these goals are harder to measure and the output less tangible than completing a marathon.

Whilst these goals are harder to measure, it does not mean we cannot have them. In fact, often, the less tangible the goal, the more important it is. Take the goal of being happier. There are ways to measure your positivity, happiness and optimism, such as on the site - https://www.authentichappiness.sas.upenn.edu. There are many questionnaires on this site which you can take at the beginning and the end of a program of action to increase any of these traits. Of course, you can measure your happiness subjectively. If you take a course of action to increase your happiness, you will soon understand whether you are succeeding in your goal or not.

There are many tools and techniques to increase your happiness, including ones that are outlined in this book. I also outlined many reasons why you should increase your happiness, including being more successful in work and life. I used the example of happiness because this is something that many people fail to set a goal around. Is it not amazing to think that many of us spend our life just wanting to be happy, yet very few people set a goal to be happy. The same goes for building up our social support, our close relationships. We know from research how important are social support is, yet very few of us set a goal to build close relationships. Again, this may seem difficult to measure, but with the short list from 1 to 10, it can be easily done. Of course, a subjective measure could be more effective.

So please understand the important of goals around some of the less tangible aspects of our life. I also hope that you can now see that by setting a success line around these goals, you will be much more motivated and inspired to achieve them. Inspiration and motivation, especially when it comes to some of the life domains that are less tangible, are by far the most important factors for success in these areas. It is often the very areas in our life where we really would benefit the most by setting goals and success lines that we fail to do so.

# Long-term goals

When you have an extended period of time to achieve the goal, it is often harder to achieve. We know that the closer we are to goal completion, the more motivated we become. Unfortunately, the opposite is usually true. A classic example is saving money for something far in the future, such as retirement. We know that due to the magic of compounding, five dollars per day at 8% return for 40 years will give you over half a million dollars. It takes you the first 20 years to get to $90,000. The next 20 years gives you $450,000. It is an experiential curve. A goal of making half a million dollars sounds ambitious; the goal of putting away five dollars per day sounds a lot more achievable. As with the compound and effect of money, when we look at goals in the long term, often a small amount of work each day reaps massive rewards. The work we do compounds over time, leading us to a life of success and abundance.

The reason we do not start saving or working towards our goals early is simple; the reward is just too far away. When setting and striving for long-term goals, we should aim to break the goals down into smaller parts with each small goal having its own success line. That way, we can celebrate our victories as we proceed along the journey. This is been proven to be a great way to maintain motivation. As we celebrate these smaller steps towards our longer term goal, not only are we happy with ourselves, but we become more confident that the longer term goal is achievable. It keeps us focused on tasks. It doesn't matter if the long-term goal is saving money, finding a life partner, becoming the CEO of your company, or renovating your home. With any long-term goal, ensure you have many short-term goals associated with it.

# Chapter 8

## Planning

*"If I had an hour to solve a problem I'd spend 55 minutes thinking about the problem and 5 minutes thinking about solutions."*
*Albert Einstein*

Now you have your dream or vision and your goals, it is time to build a plan. Think of how much time and energy you put into planning your last renovation, the new carport, the Christmas dinner or party, and think how much more important it is to properly plan your life. There is nothing more important for you, your friends, and your family. Statistically, most people spend more time each year planning their two week holiday than they do for their retirement, where they will be on holidays 52 weeks a year for many years (all going well).

*"Far too many people spend more time planning their weekends than their lives"*
*Napoleon Hill*

We plan many things especially at the micro level. We plan what's for dinner, where we have to take the kids after school, when we can drop over to see friends, and the list goes on. This planning is so important to us because the lack of action or planning in the short term has immediate consequences. If we don't plan what to make for dinner, we don't eat, if we don't plan to go to the shops, we go hungry. If we don't plan our everyday logistics, the kids complain that they missed sport, our partners complain because we didn't show up at their friend's birthday, or we get in trouble with the boss because we did not finish a task.

With long-term planning, it is too easy to put it in the "I will do it later" pile; there are so many more important, immediate things to do. All these immediate responsibilities, some important and some not so important, take precedence. If we don't make time for long-term planning today, when will we do it? If we do not take the time for long-term planning today, how will we ever ensure a successful future?

I will use a retirement example again, because all going well, we all do it. It takes long-term planning and there are a lot more research and studies done on retirement than, say, becoming proficient at playing the piano, or running a half marathon in under two hours. Although the amount of savings is one of the most critical components of being able to retire, only 49% of people ever use a retirement calculator. It is estimated, therefore, that only one out of every two people ever bother to calculate how much money they need to retire. Even fewer people ever calculate how much money they will actually have at their desired retirement age. An even more striking example of lack of planning for retirement is that only around 14% of people ever prepare a written retirement plan. On this point, I encourage everyone to make the time, over the next week, to write down a retirement plan. It does not have to be complicated; simply make some rough estimates of how much money you will have, if you keep doing what you're doing now, by the time you retire. Then estimate roughly how much you will spend each year once retired. You could simply half what you spend now and multiply that by how long you think you will live.

At this point, while writing this, I can almost feel the tension, the concern and sometimes even worse, the lack of interest in what I have just asked you to do. The reason I have tackled such a long-term, yet important task to make my point should be clear. Your retirement, your health, your goals around sports, hobbies and other interests, are yours. It is your life and you can live it any way you please. What you really need to take notice of is the fact that there are very few other people on the planet, who care about these things as much as you.

I make a point of doing my retirement calculations each year. I normally do it over a coffee on a Sunday morning. It is fun! I calculate, how much money I would need, if I stopped working that day. What would that look like? How much additional money would I need, each month to retire completely? Then I do a few calculations around if I keep doing what I am doing, what that figure would look like in 10 years. By playing around with the numbers, I gain a much better understanding of my current situation, it puts things into perspective. Of course that reality is not always something I want to see. By facing the reality of our financial situation, we are in a better position to make good decisions around work, our purchases, and other lifestyle changes.

If you do not plan your retirement, no one else will. Even if you have a financial adviser, accountant and lawyer, you are still ultimately responsible for yourself and your family. The reality is that long-term planning is often never done as it is hard to predict. The good news is that as it is so unpredictable, you do not always need to spend a lot of time on it. By simply sitting down with a coffee, pen, paper and calculator, you can often do most of the planning you need to do in a very short period of time. So when you have a mental block or resistance to making any plan, remember that an approximate plan is much more effective than no plan at all. Obviously, this follows on from what I said about retirement goals, or any long-term goals. The long-term plans, like the-long term goals, should be broken up into manageable chunks.

When planning, remember the 80/20 rule, or Pareto principle. Eighty percent of the change in your life will come from only 20% of your total effort. All things are not equal; only you know the key actions that are required to make bold and drastic changes. If you pick that top 20% correctly, you will save yourself 80% of the total work! Create the plan, just as you would plan anything. Do not think of how you are going to complete all the steps, just write them out. The important thing now is to create the plan. If it seems onerous, think of how hard it would be to succeed without one!

What you focus on expands, so plan to be doing what you love. Think of the chaos theory, or the song that says "From little things, big things grow." Major changes start in our life by simply making the decision. Like the previously mentioned captain of a cargo ship, the ship is steaming through the ocean, so much power, so much momentum, but the ship's direction can be changed by the captain simply via a tap on the keyboard or moving a lever. With your life, you already have to wake up, get dressed, eat, work, and deal with all the issues that come up. By changing your direction, you don't take up more energy. In fact, you'll find you accomplish more with less effort because you've removed the roadblocks, found your path, passion, and inspiration. It is the environment and your situation that supports your feelings, thoughts, and emotions and all these things together drive change.

*"For the past 33 years, I have looked in the mirror every morning and asked myself: 'If today were the last day of my life, would I want to do what I am about to do today?' And whenever the answer has been 'No' for too many days in a row, I know I need to change something"*
*Steve Jobs CEO of Apple computers.*

Many people fail to change because they take on too much at once. That's why it's so important to create a clear and concise plan to get there. It can be useful to start small; clean up your office, or your home, start with a moderate exercise program, or make some small changes to your diet. These small changes can help achieve bigger results as your confidence grows and you are more equipped physically and mentally to take on the larger challenges.

Look for areas where you may be able to put your time to better use; for example, give up television one night a week, or get up a bit earlier than normal. Can you do something to help yourself at lunchtime or during a break? By tackling small changes regularly, before work, lunchtime or listening to podcasts during your daily commute, you will make big progress towards successfully achieving your goals.

Remember to focus on your strengths. You gain a lot of ground in your journey by utilizing your strengths. Of course it is also good to work on and be aware of your weaknesses; however, you will accomplish more at a faster pace by leveraging your strengths. You should be selective in your goals. Do not spread yourself too thin; instead, strive for excellence in a few areas. Look for the quick wins; this is a strategy used in business and it works in our personal life too. Your strengths may not be immediately obvious to you. It is very powerful to make a list of what you're good at, your successes and your passions. This can be done in one specific area or more broadly across your whole life. It builds self-confidence and motivation. By understanding your strengths and your weaknesses, you will be ready to formulate a solid plan of action. See the strengths section for more information.

## Chapter 9

# Plan for success

*"Keep your mind fixed on what you want in
life, not on what you don't want"*
*Napoleon Hill*

Our brains give much more weight to the negative than the positive. Back on the savannahs when we were being chased by Saber-tooth Tigers, a wrong move would mean death. We have evolved to take threats very seriously. If our ancestors missed a small indication of impending danger, whether it was a Saber-tooth tiger, a snake in the grass, or a spider, they could find themselves in a very bad situation very quickly. The same went for sickness, infection, and all other natural threats. For this very good reason, our brain is hardwired to give priority to danger and threats. Research shows that our self-talk in our mind is around 80% negative and only 20% positive. Every time we think of an opportunity, we automatically start thinking of everything that could go wrong

This natural reaction may have been very useful in the past, but not so effective in our modern world. We worry about a lot of things in our world, some logical and some illogical. We worry about the judge in our mind always telling us that we may get something wrong or might not be good enough; we worry about achieving perfection, more so than is actually required; we become hyper-vigilant and super protective against the dangers that are only minor or may not even exist at all. Many times, we try to control the situation; we worry about what others will think of us or we play the victim. None of these are conducive to our success. We are very good at putting roadblocks, excuses, and obstacles in our own way. We are not so good, at planning our path to success before thinking of the negatives. We usually do it the wrong way around. We think of everything that could possibly go wrong and then try to plan a path to success through the minefield of self- imposed dangers.

## The straight path

*"I am an old man and have known a great many*
*troubles, but most of them never happened"*
*Mark Twain*

Imagine how straight the path would be to success if we planned the route first and then looked at what could go wrong? We could take a more realistic view and risk analysis of what could go wrong and actively plan to stop these things, rather than altering our course to go around them even before they happen.

Imagine how easy it would be to propel ourselves forward by planning the path in a way that we can utilize all our strengths! Rather than making our plan to include working on our weaknesses, we focus on our strengths. Like our roadblocks, excuses, and other obstacles, our weaknesses can be put aside to be dealt with separately, if at all. This idea ties into the 80/20 rule where 80% of our success will come from 20% of the effort. When we focus on the most direct path to success, when we focus on the 20% that will propel us most directly towards success, we achieve our goals naturally and easily.

Some of the most important things in life are the most simple; water, food, friends, family, etc. We are very good at complicating the simple life. Businesses can become successful by focusing on their core product or service. This technique has been used extensively all around the world to great success. When a business gets rid of the less profitable services and products and focuses on the top 20% of products or services, that give them the 80% of profit, this is when they thrive. This technique can be used very well in our own lives. By identifying the noise, roadblocks, weaknesses, and everything else that slows us down, we are in a much better position to plan around them.

Planning a straight line to success is clearly the fastest way to get there. It is simple to understand how often we do not do that by trying a little exercise. Next time you plan to do anything, whether it is big or small, make a mental note of your planning process. Did you immediately think that you would achieve what you aimed for? Or did you start thinking of the negatives? Did you immediately plan how you will achieve your goal in the fastest way possible? Did you think of how much you will enjoy the process or how much satisfaction you will gain from it? Or did you look at it more from the negative?

Please do not confuse this process with positive thinking. This is positive and proactive planning. Positive thinking assumes everything will go well. Whilst there is a time and a place for positive thinking, I'm not suggesting this is the best proven way to success. This method involves planning your route to success first and then analyzing the risks, or dangers that may be involved in that route. It means to take on different perspectives and come up with different ways in which to achieve your goal. This is the classic "think outside of the box" mindset. When you actively work to think of different ways to achieve your goal, you are building your brain muscles in a way that becomes very beneficial to you in the longer term.

By getting into the habit of actively looking at different perspectives and different ways to achieve the same goal, you are greatly increasing your chance of success. Think of the last time you were going on a drive through the city. Did you just take the first route that came to mind? When you are building a carport, doing a renovation, or a garden makeover, did you select the first plan that came to mind? When you last decided to go out to dinner with friends, did you pick the first restaurant that came to mind?

When we make decisions around the more tangible aspects of our lives, it seems common sense to look at various options and decide on the best one. We look for the best option often without examining all the negatives, we just look at positive alternatives. Often in these situations, such as driving through town, we do not plan on all the worst-case scenarios. We don't check to make sure the spare tyre has air in it, or that our roadside assistance is up-to-date, or plan what will happen if the car breaks down. Because it is something tangible and logical, it is easier to look at these things in a positive way. It is easier to assume, as we have a clear plan, that things will work out as expected.

When we are trying to accomplish something less tangible, like navigating a social situation, a job interview, making a change to our diet or exercise program, the different routes or range of possibilities become exponentially larger. We can never possibly predict, for example, all the different possible combinations or situations that may arise during a work function. If we are taking on a new project at work, the list of what could go wrong is infinite. When we are changing our diet, we can never anticipate all the different temptations, urges, and feelings we may experience. As we begin a new exercise program, it is impossible to predict how motivated or not we may be. We cannot predict all the different excuses or roadblocks we may encounter. Our brain goes into overdrive. We can lay awake at night tossing and turning, our brain going over all these different situations and combinations of what may happen. Stressing about everything that may go wrong, there is a high possibility we may not ever even start.

## Positive planning

How much more powerful would it be if we actively planned various ways to achieve our goal? How much more powerful would it be if we took some of these less tangible goals, grabbed a pen and paper, and started to write down our thoughts? If we actively mapped out the various options, then as a separate exercise, looked at all the possible issues. If on a separate piece of paper, we wrote down our objections, concerns, anxieties, and other road blocks or obstacles and then next to each obstacle, we wrote a probability between one and ten, of them actually happening; 10 being the most likely, and one being the least likely. Then for the obstacles that we deem to be likely, we then judge which ones would really affect us. If there are ones that when they occur, we can work around them at the time, or the effect will be so small it won't negatively affect us, so we can just cross them out. We work through the list and actively decide what we really need to think about, or make plans to ensure they do not happen.

How much more powerful would it be if we then review the different routes we have made towards our goal, against the real roadblocks or concerns? We decide on the best course of action and what we are going to do about the negatives. At this time, we have a clear plan, in writing, about how we are going to achieve our goal. This is positive planning. Because we have taken a proactive step to plan for the challenges ahead, because we have written clearly on paper and have worked through the

43

different scenarios, we do not need to waste more mental energy stressing over the risks.

With a positive plan, we can use our mental energy to look for and be aware of things within our environment that will help us achieve our goal. Our brain is not wasting time stressing over all the complications that may arise. Our brain leans towards the positive. We believe we can achieve the goal, because we have actively planned our way towards it.

Believing we can achieve the goal has been proven to be by far the most important psychological tool we can utilize for success. Because we believe we can achieve the goal, our conscious and subconscious mind is fully behind us and activating all the thoughts and emotions required to achieve the goal. This also includes releasing chemicals within the brain to assist us toward success. The best part however, is that by having a positive plan and having reviewed and discounted or planned around all the roadblocks that may become in our way, we can sleep at night in peace. We find serenity, energy, and motivation. We become happier and more satisfied. We are able to bring in other goals and other challenges, even if we haven't finished the prior ones.

Previously without a plan, as we take on multiple challenges, our brain just cannot keep up. We stress out, can't sleep, drink too much, smoke, eat junk food, etc. Put simply, we are overloaded with all the different combinations of possible events, issues, and roadblocks in the way. By creating a positive plan of action for each challenge or goal that we have, we are clearing our mind for success. We are also building our ability to positively plan everything in our lives. We may not need to write down a positive plan for everything we do. In fact, the more we practice, the better we get at it. We naturally start to plan in a positive way, even for the simplest things in our lives. When we write down a positive plan for more complex challenge, we become better at it.

There is a real difference between optimistic planning and pessimistic planning. Also on how we think about what happens to us as we implement these plans. I have learnt a lot about the difference from the work of Martin Seligman, the father of positive psychology, in his book Learned Optimism, and his other great books and research papers.

Wikipedia summarises his findings very well - "The benefits of an optimistic outlook are many: Optimists are higher achievers and have better overall health. Pessimism, on the other hand, is much more common; pessimists are more likely to give up in the face of adversity or to suffer from depression. Seligman invites pessimists to learn to be optimists by thinking about their reactions to adversity in a new way. The resulting optimism—one that grew from pessimism—is a learned optimism. The optimist's outlook on failure can thus be summarized as - What happened was an unlucky situation (not personal), and really just a setback (not permanent) for this one, of many, goals (not pervasive)".

Seligman elaborates on the three P's, Permanence, Pervasiveness and Personalization and explains the differences that exist between pessimists and optimists in terms of explanatory style. These explanatory styles are summarised, in Seligman's book:

- "Permanence: Optimistic people believe bad events to be more temporary than permanent and bounce back quickly from failure, whereas others may take longer periods to recover or may never recover. They also believe good things happen for reasons that are permanent, rather than seeing the transient nature of positive events. Optimists point to specific temporary causes for negative events; pessimists point to permanent causes.

- Pervasiveness: Optimistic people compartmentalize helplessness, whereas pessimistic people assume that failure in one area of life means failure in life as a whole. Optimistic people also allow good events to brighten every area of their lives rather than just the particular area in which the event occurred.

- Personalization: Optimists blame bad events on causes outside of themselves, whereas pessimists blame themselves for events that occur. Optimists are therefore generally more confident. Optimists also quickly internalize positive events while pessimists externalize them."

So when you are trying to look at you're planning from a positive perspective, or if you are evaluating events in your life, please keep in mind the three P's. By taking an optimistic view of your plans and reaction to events, you are in a lot better position to grow and be happy.

# Chapter 10

## Action

*"Do you want to know who you are? Don't ask.*
*Act! Action will delineate and define you"*
Thomas Jefferson

With a clear and detailed plan, simply enjoy the experience. There is an old proverb: *"What you hear you forget, what you see you remember, what you do, you understand."* The key is doing! Have you ever noticed the end of satisfaction is a-c-t-i-o-n? The Latin word *satis* means "enough." What the ancient Romans clearly understood was that enough action produces satisfaction. It is how you find happiness and success. Motivation is from the Latin word 'movement'. Motivation comes from action. You cannot have motivation without action. You should commit to doing something each day toward achieving your goals.

In the words of Mahatma Gandi *"The future depends on what you do today."* He did not say the future depends on what you talk about today! The real key to success in anything you want to accomplish is taking action. When this action is toward a self-concordant goal, we are more likely to succeed. So we gain motivation by chasing something that is aligned with our intrinsic interests, and values. When we really want to do something and we take action, this is when we succeed.

This is true with anything we put our mind to. For some people, they fall short because they never take any action. For other people, their issue is that they take too much action, but on the wrong thing. It is so important that we take deliberate, focused action; this is really the key to life. By taking deliberate focused action, we can achieve anything we want in a fast effective and productive way.

*"Being busy does not always mean real work. The object of all work is production or accomplishment and to either of these ends, there must be forethought, system, planning, intelligence, and honest purpose, as well as perspiration. Seeming to do is not doing."*
Thomas A. Edison

Find the right person to use as a sounding board to do it with you or be there for assistance and support. It is critical you commit to someone, to keep you accountable, and who will also be there to celebrate your victories with, big or small. You can use family, friends, or, of course, I suggest a change coach. Whoever you use, be sure that you can be open and honest with them and they will inspire and encourage you along the way.

I have used a coach myself. I find it very powerful. It forced me to articulate exactly what I wanted and what I needed to do, in order to achieve it. What I came to realize, during my coaching, was that I had never really been that accountable to anyone before. At work, I had for sure. Regarding some of my family commitments I had. When it came to my own personal dreams and desires, what I wanted out of life, not what someone else needed me to do, I had never been accountable. I never had to set goals and be accountable for them.

Try a small experiment. Think of something you want to do. Perhaps it is something that always gets put to the back of the priority list, because of work and family commitments. Set a specific plan on how you will achieve it and a time frame. Then find someone who will hold you to it and tell them what and when you are doing it. Tell them you will update them on the progress. And make some agreement if you do not do it; wash their car, do them a favor, or something fun like cooking them dinner. Then notice the difference of commitment to the task.

As you change, you gain something. As this happens, you are also losing, or letting go, of something. This loss can be hard to cope with even if you are losing something that does not benefit you. So the right support and gaining a clear understanding that this is part of the process is important. It's all common sense, but it is amazing to find out how few people have ever followed any process. So, again, I challenge you. Start now; it's time to decide, to commit, and to find your passion.

*Michael Hunt*

For those who wish to know our about how our actions affect our motivation, please read about Vroom's Expectancy Theory, developed by Victor Harold Vroom. One of the most influential books on the subject of motivation was written by him in 1964, called Work and Motivation. The theory seeks to explain why individuals make certain decisions and how their actions and motivation are affected by variables such as Expectancy, Instrumentality and Valence.

## Chapter 11

# *The Cycles of Life*

*"There are often many things we feel we should do that, in fact, we don't really have to do. Getting to the point where we can tell the difference is a major milestone in the simplification process"*
*Elaine St. James*

When you are on a role in one area, go with it, even if some of your other plans suffer. Make the most of your passion and your enthusiasm. The reward you receive from the effort asserted can be tenfold. This is why your plans need some flexibility. It is important to keep an eye out for the things that you don't need to do. When you are doing something you really don't like, think to yourself: does this really have to be done? Can I outsource it (pay someone else to do it)? Can you say no to that person? Do you really have to attend? This is especially important as you start being passionate and productive in your other activities.

As in nature, life works on cycles, both short and long term. It is much easier to complete a task, especially if you are working with passion and excitement, than to stop and start back at a later time. Much more can be accomplished with less effort if we know when we are being productive or when we are being busy for the sake of being busy. Parkinson's law is the adage that "work expands so as to fill the time available for its completion." What this law is saying is that we can work so much smarter and faster if there is pressure on us to do so, or we can take a lot longer to do a task just because we have the time to do it. Its part of the intangible nature of life that we can't always understand results or grasp how much we can accomplish with such little effort. Conversely, how could a task that should be easy ever become hard. We need to look for our natural rhythm.

Have you ever noticed, when completing a task, that it is very easy? Or alternatively, it is a lot harder than you thought it should be? These are the times it is worth taking advantage of the situation or to just cut your losses.

We need to know when we are ready or not ready, when we work at our best, when we are most creative and productive, and when we should be doing certain tasks. Some people are very productive in the morning and for some people it is late at night when the family is asleep. We have good days and bad days. This cycle of productivity or non-productivity, enthusiasm or laziness, excitement or boredom, is seen by someone who does not understand the delicate cycles of life as a hindrance and they become frustrated.

When we are trying to get things done, but are not ready or in the right state of mind, it can be soul destroying. When we are on an up cycle and have enthusiasm, excitement, and productivity, but do not understand how to put ourselves in the right environment, or realize that in this period we need to change our normal schedule or habits, this can be equally frustrating. By understanding and embracing our natural cycles and rhythms, we achieve more with less effort while still enjoying the down time. When we are tuned into the cycle, after a period of activity, we can enjoy the well-deserved rest without guilt, bringing us peace and serenity.

A good example of this phenomenon, in the context of long-term cycles, can be a career change. You may have been dissatisfied with your job for many years, even though there may be good reason for you to stay working in it. Then, one day, for reasons you may not even understand, you begin to get the urge to do something about it. Often at this point of time, you have the energy and the motivation to look elsewhere, to think about what's important, to examine the possibilities of what else you could do. Instead of fighting it off, put your energy into it, and don't wonder why or if you should be doing anything about it. You may feel driven to stay up late to update your resume, or search for new opportunities, or be more willing to talk to other people and ask questions. Embrace this up cycle. Try to maximize its full potential with an open mind. This passion to change won't last forever. The window will close and you will keep doing something that you don't love.

In this example, go for the interviews. You don't need to decide until you have an offer on the table! Too many people try to make a decision too early. They think way too much about why, if, when, and how. A better course of action would be to use the passion, the excitement, and the curiosity to fully explore all the options.

This is only an example of a long-term cycle of life. The same cycles happen in relationships, health, and your financial situation. I am not suggesting that every time this happens, you have to commit to a different course of action. I am recommending that when this happens, you take full advantage of the inspiration while you can. Explore all the possibilities, weigh up your options, and prepare a plan of action. You may even decide to create two plans and later choose which one to follow. The important thing is to get it on paper; this is the key. Whether you decide to act immediately or at a later date, you will find the research, the time, and the effort that you put in, will not be wasted. So please, look out for, and embrace the natural rhythm of life, in the short, medium and the long term. This is a very useful tool in the toolkit of life.

> *"Twenty years from now you will be more disappointed by the things that you didn't do than by the ones you did do, so throw off the bowlines, sail away from safe harbor, catch the trade winds in your sails. Explore, Dream, Discover."*
> *Mark Twain*

# Chapter 12

## Phases of Change

*"True life is lived when tiny changes occur"*
*Leo Tolstoy*

There are various phases of change. Sometimes we think for a long time before we change and this is ok and part of the process. We sometimes struggle with change, and we fall back to our old behavior, this is ok too. The important thing is to understand that this is normal, not to get discouraged and keep with the plan. If you plan to run four times a week, and you find it too hard, walk three times a week to start. It is better to make progress than to fall right back and give up.

It is completely normal when undergoing change to think about whether we are making the right decision. We want to change, but we don't want to change; the new way we think is better, but we enjoyed the old way; we want to go for a run, but we want to sit around. This is a normal part of the process and over time, you will think less about the old habits you try to get rid of and more about the new way of living. By understanding and accepting this, it will ensure you are not too hard on yourself. It is useful to understand that change does not happen overnight and the progress is important, whether small or great.

The phases of change were well researched by James O. Prochask, who was a Professor of Psychology and director of the Cancer Prevention Research Center at the University of Rhode Island. He Developed the Transtheoretical Model of Behavior Change (Sometimes called the Stages of Change Model), that showed that change is a process, involving progress through a series of stages. These stages have been incorporated into many personal (especially heath) and business related change programs. It is useful to have a look at these stages, as they show clearly that change is not something that we always just start. There is a contemplation and preparation period. There is also a relapse period, where the person resumes old behaviors. When relapsing, it is important to understand that, as per the model, the person has not failed, but will go back and re-enter the model where it works best for them. This may be straight back into action, but they may also need to go back to the preparation or contemplation stages.

The various stages, from Prochaska (and DiClemente's) Stages of Change Model ae summarised below.

- Pre-contemplation (Not Ready)- Not currently considering change: "Ignorance is bliss"
- Contemplation (Getting Ready)- Ambivalent about change: "Sitting on the fence"
- Preparation (Ready)- Some experience with change and are trying to change: "Testing the waters" -Planning to act within 1 month
- Action - Practicing new behavior for 3-6 months
- Maintenance - Continued commitment to sustaining new behavior -Post-6 months
- Relapse - Resumption of old behaviors: "Fall from grace". Revert back to a previous stage

*"The measure of intelligence is the ability to change*
*Albert Einstein*

Always celebrate your victories. As we change, we can easily forget what we have left behind and how much progress we have made. It is the wins that keep up going along the journey. They give us strength and hope. So make sure you celebrate them and remember them. Tick them off the list or whatever you need to do to track them. If it is a more complex task, you should rate your progress from 1-10 so you can see improvement, or ensure there are enough sub-tasks for you to track progress day to day. When we monitor something, we are more attached and committed to it, thus increasing our chance of success. A diary can be used to chart progress or simply used as a tool to manage day-to-day activities. It can be a cheap and extremely effective way to find peace and organization in a chaotic life.

## Chapter 13

# Using Strengths

*"The good life consists in deriving happiness by using your signature strengths every day in the main realms of living. The meaningful life adds one more component: using these same strengths to forward knowledge, power, or goodness"*
*Martin Seligman*

Now that we have a deeper understanding of the foundation, we can build in two components that support our foundation to create a solid structure on which to build our happiness and success. These two components are signature strengths and building positive relationships. First we will look at our signature strengths.

## Strengths to success

Utilizing your strengths is a fast track to success. Studies coming out of the field of positive psychology show us that people who do what they do best are three times more likely to have an excellent quality of life overall and they are happier for it. I want you to think about the last time you succeeded in something, work or play, or when you were in the zone, or flow, doing something you love. Were you drawing on your strengths or weaknesses? You can complete the signature strengths questionnaire at https://www.authentichappiness.sas.upenn.edu/. It is also available at http://www.viacharacter.org/www/The-Survey.

The result will show your 24 strengths in order. The key is to use your top 5 or so strengths to help you set and achieve your goals and to use them in everyday life to succeed and be happier. A meta-analysis study found that happiness leads to success in every domain of our lives. We also know conclusively from hundreds of studies over the last two decades that utilizing our strengths leads us directly to happiness. We succeed because we are doing what we love and doing it well.

Take an example; you are in a career change and you are deciding what to do. You have three options

1. Set up a business as a professional public speaker – You would find it interesting, it is good money, but will take some creativity and energy to get started, and you are not sure if you have it in you.

2. Work at a local non-profit that provides social services in the community. There is a real team spirit in the group, they are lot like you, and they are kind and supportive. But would you enjoy it enough to accept a little lower pay?

3. Go back to school and study to be an accountant. It will take two years and you are not sure if you would stick at the study and ultimately pass. You have always loved working with numbers and it would take a lot of work, but would be a great long-term career move.

You cannot decide what to do. It's driving you crazy, but then you have a thought, why not do the strengths questionnaire and find out your strengths. You look at the results and see your top strengths are zest, enthusiasm, creativity, and originality. Setting up a business as a professional public speaker suddenly sounds like a good idea. Alternatively, if you see your strengths are citizenship, teamwork, kindness, and generosity, then you may be best suited to the local non-profit that provides social services. This may be really satisfying and provide the meaning in life you were looking for. Or if you see your tops strengths are love of learning, diligence, and perseverance, you now think you may actually have what it takes to complete the accountancy course and may even enjoy it. So you decide to become an accountant.

In 2002, Martin Seligman, the father of positive psychology, identified six culturally ubiquitous virtues that included wisdom, courage, love, justice, temperance, and spirituality and under these broad categories he proposed 24 distinct strengths. Evidence suggests that "Utilizing strengths can also be used effectively as an intervention to promote happiness and protect against depression."[18] In addition, studies have "Revealed an association between the VIA strengths and recovery from illness."[19]

Whilst my main focus is on utilizing strengths for success, it is interesting that the benefits can be far more diverse. I have provided the complete list of these strengths and virtues, so you can start to think what your top strengths may be, and how you could incorporate them into your own life.

- Zest, enthusiasm, and energy
- Industry, diligence, and perseverance
- Perspective wisdom
- Citizenship, teamwork, and loyalty
- Hope, optimism, and future-mindedness
- Creativity, ingenuity, and originality
- Leadership
- Humor and playfulness
- Curiosity and interest in the world
- Judgment, critical thinking, and open-mindedness
- Kindness and generosity
- Gratitude
- Love of learning
- Fairness, equity, and justice
- Honesty, authenticity, and genuineness
- Capacity to love and be loved
- Spirituality, sense of purpose, and faith
- Modesty and humility
- Social intelligence
- Caution, prudence, and discretion
- Self-control and self-regulation
- Bravery and valor
- Appreciation of beauty and excellence
- Forgiveness and mercy

Using these strengths works just as well when planning hobbies, sports, and interests. If your strength is in citizenship and teamwork, you may enjoy team sports or being a member of club. If you are creative, you may find you enjoy the arts!

What about everyday life? If life is a bit flat, or you have a lack of energy and drive, look at your sports, hobbies, and interests, the things you do regularly and see if you are using your signature strengths. If you are not, look at ways to mix things up a bit to utilize your strengths more regularly.

I used to think I was lazy. I just want to sit around and relax! That was what life should be all about, yet I never had any energy. It worked against me. When I challenged myself and used my creativity, I was happier. It took me a long time to realize that what I thought I wanted to do was not actually what made me happy. I would get more energy and feel great taking on new challenges. Once I completed the strengths questionnaire and saw my signature strengths right in front of me, the penny dropped! A key part of the puzzle was solved. I began to reinterpret and better understand experiences in my life. It has made it easier to prioritize my time and energy and to better understand how the future will turn out when I make decisions. It has brought me clarity and a better sense of purpose and meaning, because I better understand my past experiences, my actions, and the consequences.

I urge you to complete the questionnaire for yourself. Think deeply about the results. How your actions and the consequence have been affected by the use, or lack of using your strengths, how you can refocus your goals to utilize your strengths, and how can you incorporate your strengths into your day to day life.

A major focus of positive psychology research is on "Strengths; patterns of thought, feeling and behavior that are energizing and which lead to maximal effectiveness."[20] Within coaching psychology literature, "Strengths use has been shown to be associated with both subjective and psychological well-being, even when controlling for the effects of self-efficacy and self-esteem."[21] An increasing number of therapists, coaches and consultants are "Using strengths based interventions with their clients.[22] I personally have used strength based coaching in my own practice and have found when a client understands and utilized his or her strengths, they are happier and more successful in identifying and reaching their goals.

Using one's signature strengths is considered to serve well-being and basic psychological needs, such as competence, autonomy, and relatedness. In one study, 240 college students completed measures of psychological strengths, need satisfaction, well-being, goal progress, and goal attainment at three time points over a three-month period. The results demonstrate that "Strengths use is associated with better greater fulfillment, provides a key support in the attainment of goals, and leads to greater satisfaction and well-being."[23]

It is clear that it is better to focus your energy on your strengths than always on improving your weaknesses. This does not mean you need to completely ignore your weaknesses; sometimes it can be very useful to understand what you're not so good at. Sometimes we do need to spend time to overcome our weaknesses. When we are planning for success however, it is beneficial to set goals and create plans that incorporate the use of our signature strengths.

# Chapter 14

## Positive Relationships

*"The single most important factor in our long-term happiness is
the relationships we have with our family and close friends"*
*Clayton M. Christensen*

Relationships are arguably, the most important thing we have in our lives. To have people who we can share our successes and our sorrows with is critical. Research confirms the importance of positive relationships. We are social creatures. It is commonly believed the reason humans have such a big brain is to navigate the complex social environment in which we live. So important is our ability to have successful social interaction, and hence such a big brain and head when we are born, is why we need to be nursed for the first few years of our lives.

Other animals are able to walk within days of being born. Humans, with our big brains and heads, struggle when we are young just to hold our head up. The complexity of our society is unquestionable. There are hierarchies in our social circles, our work, community, and our clubs. We are constantly navigating this complex social environment. Many people find that maintaining an active social life is difficult. Even the people who find it more natural often struggle with concerns about what other people are thinking or how they are perceived in the world.

Our mind is often going round and around, contemplating the entangled web of social interaction. How we are perceived by others matters. What they think of our successes and failures is important to us. The types of relationships that we have in our life are extremely important. The environments in which we live, and that includes our relationships, is what we deem to be normal. We grow into our environment and our social circle. If we spend time with people who are negative and always

59

complaining, we tend to take on these same characteristics. Conversely, when we spend time with positive like-minded people, we are in a better position to grow and thrive in our relationships and our life.

As we set our personal and work goals, make our plans, and prepare our futures, we should take careful note of the people we include in this future. These relationships have the ability to make or break our efforts for success and happiness. This is especially true when we are exploring possibilities and new opportunities. It may be easier to tolerate an unsupportive friendship or relationship when you are not striving for anything. When you discover possibilities and opportunities to enjoy a thriving life of abundance, happiness, and success, you quickly begin to see how non-supportive relationships can become major obstacles.

Relationships are all about give and take. The more we are interested in our friends, our family, co-workers, and other relationships, the more they become interested in us. We all know people who are always on the take. We may tolerate these people, but at some point, it is worth asking the question of whether they are worth your valuable time. As you transform your life to one of meaning, purpose, and passion, you will find your time to be extremely valuable. You will not want anyone who will dampen your spirits or bring negativity into your life.

As we take on new challenges, if we are a person who prefers to be alone, or work alone, we quickly find that we need to engage with other people. Some people find this problematic. The real key in successful relationships, especially for these types of people, is to find others with common interests and passions. When you surround yourself with like-minded people who have similar dreams and desires than yourself, it is easier to find common ground and enjoy productive conversations. Often we need to take a bold first step, initiate conversation, and make the effort. When we actively work to build positive relationships in our personal and work life, things become more refined as there is more meaning and satisfaction in what we are doing.

Whenever you are setting goals and creating plans, try to include as many positive relationships in them as possible. If you want to start running for example, enlist a friend or join a club. For any sport, hobby, or interest, there are often groups and organizations that you can join that will not only help you in your development or training, but will also open up possibilities for new relationships. It is the intangible nature of human relationships that makes it impossible to predict the outcome when you make an effort to reach out and connect with other people. When two or more people come together to find a solution to a common problem or a better way to achieve their team goal, they form a group consciousness, the mastermind. This mastermind, the bringing together of many minds in a common goal, has more power to resolve issues, find solutions, and discover new paths to success than the single mind on its own. There is real satisfaction with sharing new experiences with other people. Gaining feedback and alternate perspectives on our lives, challenges, and opportunities gives us much needed wisdom.

So when you are building your own personal structure for success and happiness, build in as many positive relationships as you can. Utilize your signature strengths every day and in every way possible. This way you will find the process easier and more natural. You will discover possibilities that originally may not have been obvious. You will experience results that you did not imagine. By utilizing your strengths, you will accomplish more with less effort and with more enjoyment. By building positive relationships, you will open yourself up to new perspectives, more support, better accountability, and most of all, have others to share your successes with.

*"Cherish your human connections - your*
*relationships with friends and family"*
*Barbara Bush*

# Chapter 15

## Happiness precedes Success

*"When I was 5 years old, my mother always told me that happiness was the key to life. When I went to school, they asked me what I wanted to be when I grew up. I wrote down 'happy.' They told me I didn't understand the assignment and I told them they didn't understand life"*
*John Lennon*

With a solid understanding of the foundation and structure, supported by your signature strengths and positive relationships, we now look at some inner workings of happiness and success. Happiness and positivity are our key to success; this is what we will cover now.

By better understanding the principles and the supporting research findings, we gain a clearer understanding of what it takes to be happy and successful. This deeper knowledge empowers us to discover meaning and understanding in the process. By realizing what we are doing is backed by careful science, we are more confident in the outcome. Whist the research presented is not always light reading, I urge you to apply your logic and reasoning to the information. Try to understand at a deep level how the information presented relates to you in your life.

By building your knowledge and understanding of the inner workings of your mind and the true nature of cause and effect, you will discover limitless possibilities and create a life with purpose and meaning; a positive, happy and successful life, in which you are confident of achieving what you set your mind to. Think of how many years you studied at school and possibly even college or university. The knowledge has propelled you to a better life. The time spent understanding your own life, your own inner and outer world, the nature of cause and effect, is invaluable. You will reap the rewards for the rest of your life.

So whilst I have attempted to make these pages as interesting as possible, they are a summary of some very dry research papers, study results, and information from some of the best minds on this subject across the globe. Translating this wealth of information into a light-hearted, easy to read text is not always possible. It is, however, well worth your patience.

Happiness, I propose, is the ideal state, the pinnacle of our life. With the exception of our basic needs and adequate health care, of course. Once we reach beyond these "prerequisites," everything else we do seems to lead toward our happiness, our sense of meaning and purpose. Money, a new car, a bigger house, or great holidays are all ultimately there to provide us with happiness. They enable us to have a happy and fulfilling life. So is it worth sacrificing happiness to get all these things? I would like to explore the fact that happiness that not only should be sought after first, but once we obtain it, it will actually lead us to these things, to success and prosperity.

We have been brought up to think that success leads to happiness. If we get a promotion, the new job, or a pay rise, the new house, a new car, or a new toy to play with, we will be happy. Once we succeed, we believe that will lead us to happiness. I am here to prove to you this is one of the most fundamental misconceptions of our time.

The danger of this misconception is that it has the potential to railroad our entire life. When we spend our life chasing a higher income, better car, new lounge chairs, or whatever the case may be, we are risking missing out on some of the better things in life. We are gambling our time for money. Of course we need to work to provide for ourselves and our family. Of course we want to live a comfortable existence. Of course we deserve to luxuriate in some of the finer pleasures of life. This is only normal. But what I would like to show you is that there is another way.

Before we delve deeper into the relationship between happiness and success, we should look at what makes us happy. More specifically, what makes us sustainably happy, so we are really happy deep down. What increases our well-being, so we can reach self-realization and be fully functioning?

To understand this, we should look at the two ways we can find happiness.

1. The Hedonic Approach, which focuses on happiness and defines well-being in terms of pleasure attainment and pain avoidance. This can also be called Subjective Wellbeing, and is commonly related to the feeling when you buy a new item or gain pleasure from something that is short lived. It may be eating ice cream, having a drink or eating out. It is when we are in a good mood. Hedonic pleasures do not last long. We adjust quickly to these type of pleasures. Even larger investments like a new TV, clothes or even a car. When you first buy them, you are very happy, but very soon you adjust to them. This happens also with work promotions, a new house and other big things. They are like sugar hits, and wear off quickly. We can even have withdrawals, so we feel the need to buy something else new or eat and drink more, anything to get that feeling back.

2. The Eudaimonic Approach, which focuses on meaning and self-realization and defines well-being in terms of the degree to which a person is fully functioning. Think of times in your life when you feel you belong, when you have a sense of control or autonomy. When you find meaning and purpose. Think of Maslow's hierarchy of needs, and the term self-actualization. This is Psychological Wellbeing, where we are happy at a very deep and sustainable level. This is when we want to jump out of bed in the morning, excited about the day.

This does not mean we need to avoid Hedonic pleasures, in fact they are an important and enjoyable part of life. What is useful to understand is they need to be balanced with eudaimonic pleasures that will sustain our happiness for a longer time. So when I talk about happiness and success, I am leaning toward, but not only talking about, the eudaimonic version of happiness, because this is where we really start to flourish.

By focusing on our own happiness and well-being first, success will follow. In this case, we win both ways, we are enjoying life because we are happy, and because we are happy, we are successful. There is an old saying that says "You wouldn't wish you had had more time at the office when you're on your death bed." Ultimately, life is about your relationships, your family, and friends. Life is about what you achieve and the way you achieved it. It is far too easy to say this, yet when there are bills to be paid and a family to feed, off to work we go.

If we can manage to convince ourselves that we should lean towards happiness and positivity, the rewards will come our way. How often have we seen in life that for some people things just go their way, and for others, every turn seems to be working against them? In this section, my aim is to convince you that happiness precedes success.

We all want to be successful and we all want to be happy. This chapter is about getting the order correct, that happiness leads to success, and not the other way around. We have been brought up to think that success leads to happiness. It is this belief that makes us spend so much time and energy going after money and possessions. It is this belief that makes us put so much pressure on ourselves, because we think once we succeed, we will be happy. Study after study has shown that happiness precedes important outcomes and indicators of thriving, including; fulfilling and productive work, satisfying relationships, superior mental and physical health, and longevity

My aim is to prove to you, by presenting research and studies, that happiness promotes, and is usually the precursor, to success. I do not intend to say that unhappy people cannot be successful; they can and are. Nor do I intend to give the impression that you need to be overly joyful, smiling all the time happy, to accomplish your goals. My intent is to help you understand that happiness can be used to help you succeed.

Too often at work, we put on our business face, we try to be serious, and not let our true emotions out. My hope, by presenting these findings, is you will begin to understand that by letting your happiness, your enjoyment, and optimism shine in your work and personal life, you will be more likely to succeed and achieve your goals. This is accompanied by the added advantage of better relationships, health, and longevity. When you let people at work know you are happy and even take active steps towards building your happiness, you are actually helping other people to feel happier. This in turn increases the chances of them and your team as a whole succeed.

When I was managing an office and project teams, and someone was smiling and laughing, I would often go over to them with a big smile and in a joking voice say, "Why are you laughing? You're at work. You shouldn't be happy!" This was known to the people who I worked with to mean that although I was their boss, I was pleased to see them laughing and having a bit of fun. Too often in a work environment, we are unknowingly bringing down the mood of others by putting on our business face. I hope by reading this, you can aim to be a little more natural and happy in the work environment. Happiness is infectious and the more we can promote happiness in our workplace and at home, the more successful and enjoyable our days become.

If you are not a naturally happy person, please do not despair. We know from research that everyone has a different set point, a range of happiness. Some people are naturally bubbly and energetic, while other people are naturally introverted, quiet, and a little bit less happy. For those people who are naturally less happy than the rest of us, or don't jump up a bed in the morning excited to face the day, please do not despair. The aim of this book is to give you tools and techniques to allow you to operate in your higher range of happiness. Many of the benefits outlined in this chapter can be achieved by individuals who normally are not overly happy, yet are operating in a slightly more positive and optimistic state of mind.

The research supports the notion that "It is the amount of time that people experience positive affect that defines happiness, not necessarily the intensity of that affect. Furthermore, findings from the experimental studies suggest that positive emotions can produce desirable outcomes even in the absence of a very happy disposition."[24] This same study also suggest that "Human emotional life is rich, and that the relations of positive affect and negative affect to functioning are complex ones. At times, happiness will be most adaptive and at other times may require a level of misery or at least discontent. Working towards a positive state of mind, happiness, or a feeling of general well-being, is to your advantage. This is true, independent of your genetic set point."

Over the last decade, there has been a mountain of research around this very subject. The results are conclusive; happiness leads to success, not the other way around. When we are happy, we are generally positive. This happy and positive state of mind increases our creativity, motivation, and our passion. This in turn leads to success. Conversely, if we are waiting to be happy, if we are waiting for the next success to make us happy, our performance suffers.

It is common sense when you think about it. When you are happy, you tend not to be on the defensive. Your mind is free to look for opportunities and solutions. You are future orientated and positive of the outcomes. Being happy generally means you are not spending your time looking for immediate dangers or worried about fears or other concerns. When you are happy, you tend to be more confident, optimistic, and likable. You become more flexible and you are naturally encouraged to be involved in life and to take on new challenges. The more time and the longer we are happy, the more skills and resources we build up.

When we are happy, we are more likely to be around happy people. We are more likely to increase the happiness of people around us. We only have to look around in our own lives to see that happy people tend to stick together. This is true of unhappy people too. We have a tendency to; either sit around or talk about what is wrong with our jobs and our lives, or alternately share and express the good things that are happening in our lives.

Numerous studies show that happy individuals are successful across multiple life domains, including marriage, friendship, income, work performance, and health. This has been proven using a meta-data analysis on happiness and success research from 225 papers comprising over 275,000 participants. The results reveal "Happiness is associated with, and precedes numerous successful outcomes, as well as behaviors paralleling success."[25] Many of the findings in this chapter were highlighted in this meta-data analysis study. Therefore, I wish to recognize the extensive work in this area by Sonja Lyubomirsky, Laura King, and Ed Diener. In addition the works by Barb Fredrickson on her Broaden and Build Theory. They really have proven happiness leads to success.

*"A merry heart goes all the day. Your sad tires in a mile-a."*
*William Shakespeare*

What does the research show specifically? It is this "Positive moods and emotions lead people to think, feel, and act in ways that promote both resource building and involvement with approach goals."[26] "Positive emotions signify that life is going well, the person's goals are being met, and resources are adequate."[27] In these circumstances, as the researcher Fredrickson has so lucidly described, "People are ideally situated to' broaden and build.' In other words, because all is going well, individuals can expand their resources and friendships; they can take the opportunity to build their repertoire of skills for future use; or they can rest and relax to rebuild their energy after expending high levels of effort."[28]

The research has shown us that when we are positive, we are more likely to take on new challenges and enjoy new experiences. We are more likely to build on previous experiences and knowledge to help us achieve more in the future. Barbara Fredrickson says this happens for two reasons "First, because happy people experience frequent positive moods, they have a greater likelihood of working actively toward new goals while experiencing those moods. Second, happy people are in possession of past skills and resources, which they have built over time during previous pleasant moods. This unifying framework builds on several earlier bodies of work--the broaden-and-build model of positive emotions."[29]

# Chapter 16

## Happiness at Work

*"I want to work and be happy"*
*Rickie Lee Jones*

Sigmund Freud reportedly once said, "Lieben und arbeiten," to love and to work are what a "normal" person should be able to perform well.

I had a friend who used to say "I love my Job", this has always stuck with me. Another friend, Peter, once said to me "We are at work at least 8 hours a day 5 days a week. We better find something we enjoy" What both of these people taught me, was the importance in finding work we enjoy, or if we are lucky, LOVE. If we do not enjoy, or love our work, is this not a real waste of our precious time, if not our life? How disappointing would it be to get to the end of your life, only to find that you have wasted 8 hours a day 5 days a week? Wouldn't it be so much better, if we find satisfaction and meaning in what we do?

Even if we need to go through some pain of transition, or spend time re arranging how we work, surly this is worth the effort if we end up enjoying our work more. In my experience as a manager, I have had times, when employees were unproductive and bringing the mood of the whole team down. When I took the time to understand their issue, I often found, it was not getting rid of them that was the answer. By identifying the parts of their job they enjoyed doing, and making an effort to give them more of that, I often found they experienced a complete turnaround. The small effort, on both our parts, lead to increased productivity and more importantly a happy employee.

I had an experience when I was younger, setting up and running a small telephone installation business. The business failed after a few years, not from lack of work, but too much work. The cash flow killed us in the end. We could not support all the wages and equipment costs, while waiting to be paid.

I learnt more about business in those few years than I could ever learn at collage. Yet my greatest lesson, was not about the cash flow, or operational management. I found that the very long hours, and stress of running that type of business, was just not fun! I could not really enjoy it. In fact, although there was many great times, I was really unhappy, because of the stress and long hours. I did not LOVE my job. So the failing of the business, was a blessing in disguise (an expensive one). When I wound up the business, I not only had learnt many valuable lessons but, I learnt that I needed to be doing something I enjoy. It set me free.

In addition to learning about myself, I also learnt how hard it is to be a boss and owner. From that time on, I would always work towards making the boss successful. Every day, I would ask myself; how can I work in a way that will increase profit and more importantly, not cause headaches for the boss or owner of the business?

This was my greatest insight into how to enjoy my work and succeed in my career. Yes, I said enjoy my work! Many think that the way to enjoy work is to slack off and do as little as possible, this could not be more wrong! What I found, is when I work towards making my manager look good, the boss happy and the owner profit, work was great. I would receive praise and recognition. I would receive offers of promotion and new opportunities. I found meaning and passion at work, because what I was doing helped the people around me, including the important people. When others were being made redundant, I was been given more opportunities. I wanted to go to work, and I enjoyed it, all because I was there for a purpose. The days would go fast and there was always satisfaction gained in what I did.

Many studies show that happiness leads to success at work. In one study that examined if happiness leads to success, they found that "Happy workers enjoy multiple advantages over their less happy peers. Individuals high in subjective well-being are more likely to secure job interviews, to be evaluated more positively by supervisors once they obtain a job, to show superior performance and productivity, and to handle managerial jobs better. They are also less likely to show counter-productive workplace behavior and job burnout."[30] Even before entering the workforce, "People with high subjective well-being are more likely to graduate from college."[31]

Evidence from a variety of sources shows that happy people are more satisfied with their jobs.

Once in the workforce, happy employees receive relatively more favorable evaluations from supervisors and others. For example, in one study, "Managers of happy employees of three Midwestern organizations gave them higher evaluations for work quality, productivity, dependability, and creativity. It has been found, work performance may be more strongly predicted by well-being than by job satisfaction."[32] Studies also showed that "Job performance, as judged by supervisors, was significantly correlated with well-being, but less correlated with measures of job satisfaction."[33]

This shows that well-being and happiness, in your life generally, can be more important to job performance than the satisfaction of the job itself. The evidence makes it clear that the relationship between a happy and fulfilling work life and a happy and fulfilling private life is extremely strong. Some people have a tendency to try and get through their work lives, taking the easy route, thinking somehow that working harder for the boss is giving more of themselves than they are paid for. The research in this area shows a different story.

We are creatures who actually enjoy a challenge. Too much inaction can be as harmful as too much poorly managed stress. The more we give to our work in passion and enthusiasm (not extra time), the more we enjoy it and the happier we become. The happier we are at work, the more productive we are and the better we are at it. This leads to all sorts of advantages for us, such as promotion, a pay rise, or something as simple as just keeping our job. We become more satisfied with work and in return, more satisfied with our lives in general. One study even found that "Happy cricket players had higher batting averages."[34] Another study found that "Service departments with happy leaders were more likely to receive high ratings from customers, and that the happy tone of the sales force was an independent predictor of customer satisfaction."[35]

Corroborating these results, a recent study showed that, "Happy CEOs of manufacturing companies were relatively more likely to have employees who rated themselves as happy and healthy, and who reported a positive, warm climate for performance. In turn, the organizational climate was correlated with productivity and profitability."[36] In addition to happiness, "Optimistic CEOs receive higher performance ratings from the chairpersons of their boards and head companies with greater returns on investment."[37]

This happiness and success relationship shows up time and time again in numerous studies. Including one study that showed "Happier employees were rated by their administrative officers as superior up to 3.5 years later in the four dimensions of support, work facilitation, goal emphasis, and team building."[38] To some people, this may seem odd. We are lead to believe we should work hard to succeed. This idea of working hard and being happy seems almost in conflict. We may work hard and feel satisfied, but happy? The more we understand that positive emotion and happiness actually helps us succeed, the better. It means we need not keep a serious business face, only to change to happy one when we get home. Not only do we know the happy face helps us in the work environment, but if we pretend to be serious at work, we run the risk of keeping this negative personality trait when we go home to our families and friends.

## Negotiation and conflict resolution

We know instinctively that happy people tend to get along with others better. In my 20 years' experience working in the corporate world, I had more than my fair share of experience with conflict. This conflict occurred between managers and employees, work colleagues, and even with customers. Time after time, I saw that employees who were less happy and less satisfied in work and life were the ones who created the conflict. An Investigation[39] of the CEOs of 62 U.S. companies and their top managers revealed that "Work groups whose members were high in average happiness were less likely to experience conflict and more likely to cooperate."

## Flexibility and creativity

One interesting finding that directly affects success in the workplace and in life is that happy people have a tendency to be more flexible and more creative. "Relatively higher scores on tests of creativity have been documented in happy, relaxed, and bold children."[40] Furthermore, "Eminently creative people have been shown to be characterized by dominance and self-confidence and consistently related to long-term well-being."[41]

Richards, who wrote the study, Creativity and Bipolar Mood Swings: Why the Association? researched "everyday creativity" where people find new ways to approach activities and problems in their daily lives. She found that "Everyday creativity occurred when people were in a normal or elevated mood, and rarely when they were depressed. Positive moods, particularly those involving high-arousal emotions such as excitement or joy, are also related to curiosity and desire for exploration."[42]

The laboratory findings on induced positive moods suggest that "Pleasant emotions enhance performance on simple measures of flexible thinking and originality. The association might be due to the fact that positive moods make the person feel safe and secure, and therefore, lead him or her to think in more divergent ways, without feeling threatened, in other words, to be more playful."[43]

In the modern workplace, we are often called upon to be flexible and find creative solutions to problems. This flexibility and creativity are much sort after traits for a wide variety of work functions. By using these traits, we are able to complete complex tasks more efficiently, making our work more interesting, rewarding and, in some cases, more lucrative.

# Chapter 17

## *Happiness and Social Relationships*

*"Relationships constitute the single most important factor
responsible for the survival of homosapiens"*
*Ellen Berscheid - The Human's Greatest Strength: Other Humans*

Berscheid highlighted the centrality of social relationships to successful human functioning. The fact that individuals who are happy and are more satisfied with life have more friends and more social support, as well as experience happier interpersonal relationships, is one of the most robust findings in all the literature on success and flourishing.

We all know how much better it is to be around positive, happy people as compared to sitting around with people who complain about everything. Sure, we all like to vent our frustrations sometimes. Here we are really talking about people who are always negative. Those who cannot break away from the negative talk and say something positive. These are the people who bring us all down. The research supports this. One study showed how "Happier individuals are more likely to be rated as energetic and active by their families and friends."[44] Happier people are generally more knowledgeable because they are usually more curious and willing to learn.

In a 6-year, four-panel study of Australians, "Participants' individual happiness at earlier time periods increased the likelihood that they would have a happy marriage at later time periods."[45] When we do say something negative, it often takes many positive comments before the person feels better, or the situation is resolved. We cannot say something negative to a friend and think we can just say sorry, or counteract it with something positive and all will be forgiven. It takes time. There is a ratio of how many positive comments vs negative we make. We need to make a lot more positive comments, or have many more positive conversations than negative, if we want our relationships, with friends or our partner flourish. One study further reinforces this view by proving "The longevity of marriages is best predicted by the ratio of positive versus negative interactions."[46]

## Likability

Happy people are generally more likable. Generally speaking, unless we look to be unhappy, we enjoy being around people who are happy. They lift our mood and make us smile. This is partly due to our mirror neurons, that we touch on latter. The research in this area shows an even broader picture. Research has shown that "Happy and satisfied individuals are judged as more physically attractive, more intelligent and competent,"[47] more "friendly, warm, and assertive,"[48] and "less selfish."[49] A study by Diener and Fujita found that "Friends and family members of happy students, relative to those of less happy ones, rated them as more socially skilled (e.g., more articulate and well mannered), better public speakers, self-confident, and assertive, and as having more close friends, a strong romantic relationship, and more family support."[50]

*"The good life, as I conceive it, is a happy life. I do not mean that if you are good you will be happy; I mean that if you are happy, you will be good"*
*Bertrand Russell*

Individuals who score high on happiness report a "relatively greater interest in helping people,"[51] and a tendency enjoy "sharing or helping others."[52] In summary, happy people are not only more likable, but they are better liked by others.

## Social Support through strong relationships

All successful people have strong social support through business and personal networks. Whether you're running a business, a family, and/or trying to live a fulfilling and happy life, a solid social and business network is critical. Our friends and other relationships are there to celebrate our victories and help us overcome and make sense of our defeats. Our social support is the most important, yet one of the least tangible resources we have in life. Besides counting the amount of Facebook friends, LinkedIn contacts, or how many people show up to our birthday party, it is very hard to definitively calculate the size, depth, and nature of our social support. Our social and business network is built up over time by mutual assistance, understanding, and respect. We should never underestimate the power of our social and business networks to help us succeed.

In the workplace, happy employees have been found to "receive more emotional and tangible assistance from both coworkers and supervisors."[53] We also see this in life, in our clubs, sporting groups, and social interactions. Even in earlier life, the "The happiest college students (the top 10%) have been shown to have high-quality social relationships."[54]

Happy people are better able to develop social relationships and build a rich network of support. To quote an often cited research on well-being, "Perhaps the most impressive single finding lies in the relation between happiness and successful involvement with people."[55].

We all know how important family is; we say blood is thicker than water. Of course family is important; we have a long term and deep relationship with our immediate family. Sometimes the bond is very strong and supportive, sometimes not so much. Even if our family is very supportive, sometimes they know us a little differently from or friends. In some ways, they know us better and in some ways, less than our closest friends. It is a different relationship. Strong relationships have been consistently shown to be one of the strongest factors in someone's success and well-being. This is relationships with family and with friends. A meta-analysis of 286 studies showed "The quantity and quality of contacts with friends was a strong predictor of well-being, even stronger than that of contacts with family members."[56]

# Chapter 18
## Happiness and Health

*"If you don't think your anxiety, depression, sadness and stress impact your physical health, think again. All of these emotions trigger chemical reactions in your body, which can lead to inflammation and a weakened immune system. Learn how to cope, sweet friend. There will always be dark days"*
*Kris Carr*

Traditionally, literature on physical and mental well-being focuses on the negative. We are told that we shouldn't smoke, drink too much, or eat fatty foods. We are told we need to exercise more and eat healthy foods. Most studies examine the effect of stress, depression, and anxiety. There are many studies telling us what will happen if we have a poor diet or drink too much or smoke. There are considerably less studies done on how happiness, hope, and optimism can have a positive effect on our lives. By building these characteristics, utilizing the structure of success, and the tools at the end of this book, we are focusing on what is right with us rather than what is wrong with us.

As we build a life of meaning and satisfaction, full of the positive things of life, we naturally rely less on some of the negative things we use currently. One study shows "Happy individuals are also less likely to engage in a variety of harmful and unhealthy behaviors, including smoking, unhealthy eating, and abuse of drugs and alcohol,"[57] in fact, many studies prove the same. In addition, if we choose to drink less, stop smoking, have a better diet, etc., we are more motivated to make the change, because we have discovered a life of abundance and meaning. We want to make the most out of our life, not just waste it away.

In a study, Optimism and Depression as Predictors of Physical and Mental Health Functioning, "Happy people consistently report themselves as healthier. Relative to their less happy peers, happy respondents rate themselves higher in global health."[58] In the meta-data analysis study mentioned at the beginning of this chapter,[59] "Happiness is positively correlated with indicators of superior mental and physical health. Happiness likely plays a role in health through its effects on social relationships, healthy behavior, *(Lower)* stress, *(Lower)* accident and suicide rates, and coping, as well as possible effects on immune function."

Research evidence reveals that "Chronically happy people are relatively more energetic and more involved in a variety of social, recreational, occupational, and physical activities."[60] In addition to its links with higher levels of activity and energy, one study Physical and Psychological Predictors of Exercise Dosage in Healthy Adults showed "Happiness is positively correlated with higher levels of physical exercise."[61] Happiness, positivity, and an optimistic perspective on your training program make all the difference. Think of how hard it is to get out of bed, to go for a run when you are unhappy, negative, and do not think that your running is sustainable. Conversely, if you have a clear plan, like running on Mondays, Wednesdays, and Saturdays for 7 km, you have a clear goal. Like if you are running a half marathon in a few months' time, and you talk with your friends and family in a positive way about this program, how much more likely are you to stick with it? Exercise is definitely one of those activities that takes a positive mental attitude.

For this very reason, please make sure you enjoy the exercise that you do. Whilst enjoying it might not be the right word for some, at least find something that you are interested in and that will keep you motivated. If you do not like running, try swimming, or a local boot camp. Exercise should be approached with the same planning and logic as any hobby or interest. The more passion you can conjure up to proceed with your exercise, the easier it will become. Find a friend to exercise with. Join a sporting club, training program, dance class, or anything else you are interested in.

The happier and more positive you are when exercising, the less you will think about the pain or discomfort. Studies have shown that "Individuals induced into a happy mood have shown relatively higher pain thresholds."[62] We also know happy people have "lower blood pressure reactivity to a stressful task."[63] Happy moods also promote health by boosting self-efficacy and optimism. This is actually self-evident when you think about it. How often, when we are happy, do we decide to take on a new challenge or do something just for the fun of it? Conversely, how often, when we are feeling down or unhappy, do we cancel a commitment, decide not to go to something, or just don't feel like taking on a new challenge?

## Immunity

One of the less obvious advantages of happiness is the boosting of our immune system. Initially, this seemed a little farfetched. Then, I started thinking of people at work who used to be sick often as compared to the people who rarely took a sick day and always seemed to be in good health. In retrospect, the happier people around the office were the ones who never had sick days and usually were in good health. Conversely, the unhappy people always seem to catch the colds.

The research Pryce-Jones conducted with her team at iOpener showed "The happiest employees [were] taking 66% less sick leave than those who are least happy". Other research gives us some data to prove, that it is not just a positive attitude to work that motivates them to go to work. Their happiness actually builds up their immune system. "Healthy volunteers were exposed to a rhinovirus and monitored for host resistance to the common cold. Those with a positive emotional style, that is, who typically said they were happy, were relatively less likely to develop a cold."[64] In a study assessing immune function directly, "Cancer survivors with more uplifts than hassles showed enhanced NK cell activity [these are the healthy cells, NK stands for Natural Killer] 18 months later."[65]

*"I believe that music in itself heals and that everything is about the power of the mind. I thought if you are happy, you don't get ill. Your health is in your head. When you are satisfied with your work, you don't get ill."*
*Andre Rieu*

## Long-term health advantage

Not only does happiness help us build our immunity and good health in the short term, it also has long-term advantages. In a study of close to

5,000 individuals, "Happiness was related to relatively better health (as measured by self-reported health problems, days missed that were due to illness, and hospitalization) 5 years later."[66] The experience of positive mood "Predicted a lower incidence of stroke 6 years later, especially in men."[67] One interesting study discovered "Happy hockey players even showed less sports-related injuries during the course of a season."[68] I find it amazing that some of these results do not reflect our general perception of happiness. We do think of happy people having more friends, for example, but not as often as the health benefits. As we discover the increasing evidence on the benefits of happiness, we should realize the importance in building our own happiness and positivity.

Optimism is another trait that helps us to succeed in health outcomes. Studies have shown "Optimism, was also associated with lowered incidence of cardiovascular disease (e.g., heart attacks and angina) 10 years later,"[69] with "Higher quality of life, heightened physical recovery, and quicker return to normal behaviors 6 months following cardiac surgery,"[70] plus "Better risk reduction for cardiovascular heart disease 8 months after surgery;"[71] all very compelling reasons to increase our general perception towards building our happiness.

I spoke about optimism and the three P's in the Positive Planning chapter (9). If you want to enjoy long term health advantages, powered by optimism, I recommend reading more, and better understanding these explanatory styles

## Longevity and survival

Of course, longer term better health can affect longevity. A number of studies have shown that happy people are less likely to die of certain causes. Even for people not naturally happy, building a more positive outlook helps. It helps us reduce heart disease, but also reduces accidents and injuries. In a study of more than 37 nations, "Subjective well-being was negatively related to automobile fatalities."[72] Also, a study of Scandinavians found that "Over a 19-year period, dissatisfaction with life predicted fatal unintentional injuries as well as intentional injuries."[73] Certainly these studies and others, like the previously stated reduction of sports injuries in hockey players, shows us that the intangible nature of happiness is often not recognized. Regardless of these studies, I am sure you would agree that it is better to have a happy life, even if it was slightly shorter, than a long miserable one!

Previously, research on the influence of emotions on longevity has primarily stressed the role of negative emotions in decreasing survival times. However, studies have also demonstrated longer survival times after an illness for people with positive emotional traits. "Women experiencing a recurrence of breast cancer who reported joy, were more likely to survive 7 years later."[74] I understand talking about joy and breast cancer in the same sentence may sound a bit strange, yet for those who are going to survive another seven years, they really do need to make an active decision on whether to get on with life or dwell on the negative. It has also been found that "Those individuals with spinal cord injuries reporting greater satisfaction with their lives were more likely to survive 11 years later."[75]

Some other really interesting findings regarding longevity have come out. It was shown in one study that "Individuals with positive self-perceptions of aging lived on average 7.5 years longer than those with less positive perceptions, even after controlling for age, sex, socioeconomic status, loneliness, and functional health."[76] Notably, the effect of positive aging attitudes surpassed the effects for body mass, smoking, and exercise.

This links into the structure for success. When we have longer term goals and dreams of what we want to be doing as we get older, we prepare ourselves for this reality. We build resources; this may be money, but also hobbies, and interests. We are clearer on where we would like to live and as we get older, we get ourselves prepared for this eventuality. We build our plans, so we discover a more positive perspective towards our aging. Compare this to someone who puts their head in the sand. Someone who just keeps working as hard as possible, without building any interests or plans for what they will do when they retire.

My own father was a pharmacist. He ran a successful business and was well loved in the community. His work was his social life. He knew his customers well. He shared their life's ups and downs, their successes and of course, their sicknesses. We tried hard for many years to encourage him to build a social life outside of work. Because he was so social at work, he never had a compelling reason to do so. When the time came to retire, he thought how great it would be to finally relax. Unfortunately, like happens with so many retirees, this relaxing was not what he really needed. Of course, after a long life of work, this sounds sensible. The reality for many, like my father, is once the meaning and purpose they derived from work is gone, they have little to live for. Their social support is suddenly gone and there is little reason to get out of bed in the morning.

My father passed away a handful of years after retirement. I have little doubt, like so many others, he would have had a long and satisfying life after work if he had actively built up his social support, hobbies, and interests outside the work environment before he retired. What we all need is to have a life outside work; a reason to live. The more meaning and purpose, and the more happiness we gain from this reason, whatever it is, the better. In a study of older individuals, "12% died over the course of 2 years, but those rated as happy were significantly less likely to die than those rated as unhappy."[77] Furthermore, researchers investigated predictors of longevity in a sample of 268 older adults. To control for age effects, the author examined the number of years a person had survived compared with the number of years he or she would be expected to live.

Of importance, "The objective happiness rating was the second strongest predictor of longevity, weaker than work satisfaction, but stronger than physical functioning and tobacco use."[78] Corroborating these findings for the link between happiness and longevity, one study showed that a "70-year-old man, of average health is expected to live 20 months longer, if he reports being satisfied with his life one standard deviation higher than his peers."[79]

Isn't it interesting that happiness was the second strongest predictor of longevity. Work satisfaction is the first. If this is not motivation to restructure or change your work, to ensure it is engaging and satisfying, I do not know what is! Of course, as previously discussed, building life satisfaction builds work satisfaction and vice versa. We do, however, need to be building both, so they have a chance to promote each other. It is no use having high work satisfaction (highest predictor of longevity) without high life satisfaction (second highest predictor of longevity) and vice versa.

In one famous study, often referred to when talking about the link between happiness and longevity, a group of researchers studied the autobiographies of Roman Catholic nuns. "Higher levels of happiness expressed in these autobiographies written at an average age of 22, were associated with a 2.5 fold difference in risk of mortality when the nuns were in their 80s and 90s."[80] They lived 10 years longer on average! The amazing thing about this study is that the nuns all lived together, ate together, and did about the same amount of exercise. This shows strongly how happiness is a precursor to successful longevity

Studies examining optimism parallel these results. For example, "Optimism was associated with lower risk of death for 800 patients followed for 30 years,"[81] and "Men with an optimistic explanatory style were less likely to die of coronary heart disease 10 years later."[82]

What we have seen is that spending time and effort to increase your happiness is not only good for an enjoyable day, but beneficial in a whole range of life's domains. These results show advantages of happiness most of us, including myself, would not have previously thought about. It is amazing to think how our long-term health can be improved just by being happy? You are enjoying life more, and with better health. This is truly a win-win situation.

# Chapter 19

## *The Broaden-and-Build Theory*

*"Broaden-and-build theory is notable for drawing explicit attention to the positive and showing that insights result when we do something more than simply look at the absence of the negative"*
*Barbara Fredrickson*

The broaden-and-build theory is one of the cornerstone works from researcher Barbara Fredrickson. The theory shows how positivity broadens our perspective and our opportunities. This broad perspective builds an upward spiral of success. In Fredrickson's own words, "The broaden-and-build theory posits that experiences of positive emotions broaden people's momentary thought-action repertoires, which in turn serves to build their enduring personal resources, ranging from physical and intellectual resources to social and psychological resources."[83] Or as Wikipedia states regarding Fredrickson, "Her main work is related to her broaden-and-build theory of positive emotions, which suggests that positive emotions lead to novel, expansive, or exploratory behavior, and that, over time, these actions lead to meaningful, long-term resources such as knowledge and social relationships."

The studies within this theory show that positive emotions give us a wider range of possibilities. As we broaden our attention and our focus, we notice and experience more of what we need to succeed. This wider focus and success builds up our resources, such as work, social, or physical. As we build up these resources, we are able to take on more challenges and overcome additional obstacles.

The research has shown that "Positive affect—by broadening exploratory behavior in the moment—over time builds more accurate cognitive maps of what is good and bad in the environment. This greater knowledge becomes a lasting personal resource."[84] What this means is that even if the feeling of happiness may be transient in nature, the resources that we acquire whilst experiencing the happiness, can be stored away and used at a later date.

Fredrickson and her colleagues have shown that "Positive affect at initial assessment, predicts increases in well-being several weeks later, in part by broadening people's mindsets"[85] and "Building their psychological resources."[86] This theory is useful, because it allows us to understand the importance, when we are feeling positive, to build our social relationships, knowledge, skills, and expertise. These resources will not only help us at the time, but be invaluable in the future, even in times where we are not feeling as positive.

## Upward and downward spirals

Upward spirals of positive emotions work like the snowball effect. We may start with a small amount of positivity, which builds and builds over time. As we turn our minds towards the positive, we notice and attract more positivity in our life. We attract more positive situations as we build our positive resources. This upward spiral of positivity has the ability to counter downward spirals of negativity. We do not have to look far, in success literature or the science of the mind, to see comments such as, "what you focus on expands", or "you are what you think." There are many others. As we set our mind on the positive, positivity builds and grows within our life.

Research indicates, that "Initial positive emotional experiences predict future positive emotional experiences, in part by broadening cognition, positive coping repertoires and increasing interpersonal trust."[87] This happens in much the same way as the broaden-and-build theory.

Positive emotions are emotions of abundance and success. As we become increasingly aware of the expanding possibilities in our life, we are energized and transformed in a way that allows us to identify limitless possibilities. This enables us to enjoy deeper social connections and build emotional resources.

Insights from the broaden-and-build theory suggest "Upward and downward spirals are not mirror opposites that simply trade negative content for positive content. Rather, consequential structural differences set them apart. Whereas downward spirals lead to narrowed self-focus and rigid or stereotyped defensive behavior, upward spirals lead to increased openness to others and novel or spontaneous exploratory activity. In effect, upward spirals are more open, permeable, flexible and social than downward spirals."[88]

So please remember, when you take action towards a positive aim, you are not only increasing your positivity for that moment, you are building positivity for the future. This is also true for the negative. We should catch ourselves when we find we are leaning towards the negative. This only leads to a downward spiral. Instead, we should always aim to ride the upward spiral of positivity towards successful outcomes.

# Chapter 20

## Positive intelligence

*"IQ, EQ and SI are three sides of the two dimensional triangle,*
*and positive intelligence provides the third dimension"*
*Shawn Achor*

There is a term, Positive Intelligence. It is explained in detail in Shawn Achor's book, Before Happiness. Shawn is a researcher and corporate trainer who has taken his training extensively around the world. He was a professor at Harvard for over a decade. His TED talk has become one of the most popular of all time with over 12 million views. https://www.ted.com/talks/shawn_achor_the_happy_secret_to_better_work?language=en

He uses scientific studies and research to support his belief that positive intelligence is more important than intelligence quotient (IQ), emotional intelligence (EQ), and social intelligence (SI). Shawn presents the hypothesis that IQ, EQ, and SI are three sides of the two dimensional triangle and positive intelligence provides the third dimension that makes the prism. He shows through research, that although in the corporate world IQ, EQ, and SI are usually the factors used to determine a new employee's abilities, these abilities are only slightly significant. Positive intelligence, he says, is the most important factor by far.

Positive Intelligence is what allows us to use all our other intelligences. Studies have shown that IQ only accounts for around 20% of someone's success. Other studies show the same for EQ and SI. Someone with a high IQ who does not have any drive or motivation to use their intelligence is of no advantage in the workplace. The same goes for EQ, and SI.

Where we see people excelling at work and in their personal life is when they have a deep appreciation of what they are doing. When they believe what they are doing has meaning and purpose. When they know what they are trying to achieve and why. When these people have a clear understanding of their personal and career goals, they are unstoppable. This is Positive intelligence. Someone who has high positive intelligence can utilize all their other intelligences. They can understand their strengths and know what resources are available to them, internal and external, to achieve their ultimate goals.

Shirzad Chamine wrote the book, Positive Intelligence, and was previously CEO of the largest coach-training organization in the world. He supports Mr. Achor's claim that positive intelligence rules supreme.

Positive intelligence gives us the ability to use our IQ, EQ, and SI to maximum advantage. It is a way to look at all situations in a positive and enthusiastic manner. By increasing our positivity, we are in a better position to use our intelligence.

Researcher Carol Dweck has a different slant on positive intelligence. This is one of Mindset. In her book Mindset – The New Psychology of Success, she suggests there are two main Mindsets.

1.-The Fixed Mindset - This mindset grows out of the belief that our basic qualities can never be changed.

2. The Growth Mindset - This mindset grows out of the belief that our basic qualities are things we can cultivate through effort; the hand you're dealt is just the starting point for development.

Most important, she shows how we can learn to use the growth mindset at any stage of life.

The real good news, is that we are not limited to how smart we are, or how much we know. We did not all go to university. We do not all have extensive work or life experiences. What we can all do is build a growth mindset or utilise our positive intelligence, to amplify the knowledge we already have. By understanding it is not just what we know, but how we put it to use that is important, we can achieve so much more than we may have originally thought.

## Positivity and Enthusiasm

When it comes to success, one of the greatest factors is our positive perspective on achieving our goals. It has been shown that once our chances of success in a goal are above 70%, we are much more likely to succeed.

Also as we get closer to the completion, or the achievement of that goal, we speed up, become more excited and confident that we will achieve it. Think of mountain climber as he gets closer to the summit or a marathon runner as he draws closer to the finishing line. This is why it can be valuable to break complex gaols into smaller parts. We can take advantage of the excitement and enthusiasm as we reach completion of each goal.

In many work environments, as it is true in life, we already have the skills we need to achieve our goals. We already have our support from co-workers, bosses, family, and friends. The deciding factor therefore is our motivation, enthusiasm, and commitment to the task.

University of Pennsylvania professor Martin Seligman, considered the father of positive psychology, did some research at MetLife. He discovered that the top 10 percent of optimists at MetLife Inc. outsold the others by 90 percent. MetLife then begun to hire for a positive mental mindset. The new agents outsold their more pessimistic counterparts by 21 percent the next year and by 57 percent the following year.

I spent decades running teams of engineers. The work was highly technical and challenging. What everyone knew is that engineers had to have a high level of expertise. If I started a junior engineer, it would take years before he could complete complex projects with minimum supervision. Once an engineer reached a certain point, when their technical knowledge had risen to a point where they could take on ordinary tasks, there was a quantum shift in what traits the most successful engineers showed. The engineers who worked on the biggest and most exciting projects, who got to choose the specific jobs and customers they wanted to work with, were the ones who were positive and enthusiastic.

The more positive and enthusiastic the engineers were, the more they believed they could find the solution, or complete the complex installation, and the more chance they had of success. This positivity allowed the engineers to complete the more complex work, therefore building their skill level. The greater the skill level, the more positive and confident they were in a task. This was in stark contrast to the engineers who harbored a negative attitude or who were unenthusiastic. The engineers who are negative would rarely take on a real challenge. They were less likely to study a manual and try out a process that they have not attempted previously. They were less likely, to put their hand up for a project or a difficult fault.

They were always choosing the easy option. This ultimately leads to a very flat learning curve. Years would go by without really getting ahead. It is the nature of technology that engineers need to be heading up a steep learning curve just to keep up with the latest technology, ultimately leaving the more negative and less confident engineers behind. I have seen far too much potential wasted by poor attitudes.

Most people in their jobs, when asked, would say they can do their jobs fairly well. Most people would understand where to go for help or who to lean on for support. Yet so many people fail to enjoy success in their careers. They are either bored, because they are not challenging themselves enough, or frustrated because they are not given (or know how to find) what they need to succeed.

Too often, we fall victim to circumstance. This can be due to many factors. It may be due to lack of training, a bad boss, and not enough resources, equipment, space, time, the list goes on. Have you noticed when these things happened to people in the workforce, there are generally two distinct approaches people will take? The first is that they will whine and moan, they will complain to everyone about how bad this situation is or how impossible it is to complete their tasks. The second approach is where people take on the challenge, make a plan, and get on with it.

I fully understand that too often, we are put in a difficult situation by our boss, our company, or our work colleagues. It does not seem fair does it? It seems like everything is working against you and you alone are the victim. I am not for one minute suggesting this does not happen. In fact, from my experience, since the Globe Financial Crisis (GFC), there have been massive cutbacks in almost every company, organization, and government department in almost every country of the world. We are in a different work reality than we were before. The challenge we have in this change of reality is not the actual reality we find ourselves in. The real challenge we have is to adjust to this reality and find ways to make it work for us.

As with the engineers who worked with me, the perspective and attitude is what makes the difference. The bankers, who survived the GFC, who got back on their feet, and got on with the job, were not necessarily the smartest. The businesses that recovered fastest did not necessarily have the best talent. The workers who either escaped retrenchment, or secured a job quickly after, did not necessarily have the highest IQ or skill in their trade. The difference between success and failure came down to attitude and perspective.

Why did this happen? Studies have used equipment to monitor where the eyes of people in front of a computer screen are looking. Researchers[89] found that negative people tended to look at the middle of the screen. Positive people, on the other hand, tended to look all over the screen. Positive people are better able to look for different perspectives and opportunities. It has been shown in research that positive people, when faced with a difficult situation, are better able to think of, and evaluate multiple options and make a better choice which will get them to their goal quicker. On a less tangible note, research by Joseph Banks Rhine on Extra Sensory Perception (ESP) showed a much greater chance of success in ESP studies when participants were fresh and excited about the results.

Although we may not be in a GFC now, we certainly are in a challenging business world. Money is tight, support is slim, and often our help is only on-line and self-generated. This can lead to a very frustrating and potentially unfulfilled work environment. Like during the GFC, there are those who will prosper and those who will not. It all comes down to an individual's positivity and enthusiasm.

# Chapter 21

## Positive and Negative Emotions

*"Your intellect may be confused, but your emotions will never lie to you"*
*Roger Ebert*

It is only natural to have both positive and negative emotions. In fact, it is an important part of life to experience both. We are in a constant state of emotional change. We can be positive one moment and negative in the next. The better we understand and notice these states, the better chance we have to control them. Whilst it may seem natural to "go with the flow" and just let "what will be, will be," We also know how quickly things can go backward when we let the negative emotions take over.

I was always a "go with the flow kind of guy." In fact, despite my studies, I am still a bit like that. The difference now is that I recognise the difference between accepting the situation I have put myself in verses ending up somewhere that just happened without any sort of plan.

Negative emotions are more powerful, more dominant, than positive ones. It is assumed this is due to the way we have evolved. In past times, we were in much greater danger if we ignored a bad feeling or a sound in the bushes, when we may have been attacked by a saber tooth tiger or other such tragedy. As previously noted, 80% of our self-talk is negative. So as the negative emotions and thoughts are so powerful, it is important for our positivity to actively build our ability to see the positive. This is not to convince ourselves of a reality that does not exist, only to see it as it is. We need to see the true nature of a situation if we want to make the best decisions and take the most advantageous actions. "Human experience is dynamic, as individuals continually adjust their behavior to the demands of day-to-day living. This need to adapt to changing and challenging circumstances is inevitable, a constant fact of life, out of which emotions arise."[90]

A more technical description from a paper co-authored by Barbara Fredrickson is "'Negative emotions, in particular, can become a source of dysfunction. Such negative emotions also often co-occur with dysfunctional social interactions, which can perpetuate psycho physiological reactivity and trigger destructive behavior toward self and others. Conversely, positive emotions such as joy, amusement, hope, and awe themselves multi-component response systems can serve as a bulwark against the stress of life."[91]

Research and studies clearly support these views. In a wide variety of experiments, "Induced positive emotions, relative to induced neutral and negative states, broaden the scope of people's visual attention,"[92] "eye-tracking,"[93] this is what I mentioned before about positive people looking all over the screen, and" brain imaging."[94] "Induced positive emotions also expand people's repertoires of desired actions,"[95] positive emotions increase participants "creativity,"[96] and their "openness to new experiences."[97] The evidence is mounting that positive emotions broaden people's attention and thinking in both personal and interpersonal domains.

As you can see, there has been much research in this field. The science is clear about the advantages of positive emotions. You should be able to identify experiences in your own life when you were very positive about something and it went well, or, in contrast, when you were negative about something and it did not go so well. When a physical change, such as fitness, is shown to benefit us, we feel the need to increase our fitness. We now know the importance of positive emotions so the same rigor should be attached to increasing these types of emotions. This is where we can greatly increase our chance of success. Admittedly, the connection between emotions and success may not seem solid and tangible without the evidence, as we are not accustomed to thinking our emotions assist us in our daily lives. This is the thinking we need to overcome. By understanding the concepts and the evidence of which they are based, we can take advantage of a hidden power that is not obvious to many people.

# Positive Inception

The term positive inception is a concept promoted by Shawn Achor. In essence, it means to inspire others with your positivity. When we build our own positivity and others see it, they are naturally motivated and inspired. As we help others, we are also helping ourselves in two ways. Firstly, we feel good by helping another person. Secondly, and possibly even more important, as the other person builds their own motivation, they naturally reflect that energy back to us. This is the classic upward spiral of positivity. We help others and that in turn helps us. Think of a simple example like if you decide to take up running. As you become more motivated and inspired to train, you naturally inspire your friends to start their own exercise program or join you when running. If they become motivated and join you running, there are obvious advantages. You will automatically have an accountability partner; someone who is mutually committed to the training program; someone who will congratulate you and inspire you when you make it to training and alternately notice when you do not show up. Even if your friend decides to take up a different sport or activity, you will have someone to talk with about your training, your progress, and vice versa.

The concept of positive inception is as beneficial in the work environment or in other life domains. If you inspire and motivate others at work, you build a deeper relationship with that person. They are more likely to assist you when required or simply show an interest in your progress. The importance of deep social connections is undeniable in work and our own personal life. The more positive your reality becomes, the more you naturally create a more positive environment for everyone around you. This in turn increases everybody's chance for success.

*"If you are successful at creating a positive reality but incapable of sharing it with others, then that reality will be limited and short lived, but by utilizing the techniques of positive inception, you can create a renewable source of positive energy for you and the people around you"*
*Shawn Achor*

# Chapter 22

## Leaning into the Beat

*"Life is one grand, sweet song, so start the music"*
*Ronald Reagan*

Musicians know they can change the feel of the music by leaning forward or backward on the beat. Someone musically inclined should find this section makes a lot of sense. For those who are less versed in the art of music, but would still like to understand where I'm going with this, I'll give you a little experiment. First you need a beat. You could have a friend clap, use a metronome, a very loud clock that you can hear the second hand, or if you really coordinated, you can use your feet to make the beat. Once you feel the rhythm and the beat and can anticipate where it's going to land, start clapping with the beat. So far so good. Now, begin to clap just ever so slightly after the beat. Be sure not to lose rhythm or be so slow that the regular beat catches up to you. Experiment with how you feel and how the sound feels when you clap slightly behind the regular beat.

Now do the same exercise, except try to clap slightly before the beat, only just in front of the regular beat, like you know when it is going to come so you anticipate it slightly. Play around with both, leaning into the beat, and back away from the beat. What we find in music is that if you start to clap just in front of the beat, the sound and the feel of the music becomes slightly rushed. When you lean back on the beat slightly, the music sounds slightly mellow or relaxed. You are not clapping faster or slower than the beat, you are still keeping time, but with a slight emphasis on where your clap is in relation to the set beat. This is an interesting exercise, because although the music is relaxed or rushed, you are not losing the rhythm or time with the beat.

This can be used as an analogy for life. Sometimes we try to be ahead of our natural rhythm. We try to anticipate every move and to lean slightly into our day. Our heart and mind tend to race a little more and the day feels rushed. This is not a bad thing; in fact when I have a lot to do, and it is a big, busy day, I find the extra adrenaline, stress, and sense of urgency a useful driving force.

Once we understand the concept, it is crystal clear that we are actively running slightly ahead of our natural rhythm. Conversely, when we are leaning slightly back, almost following the rhythm of our day, this can feel more mellow or relaxed. Please do not confuse leaning back on the natural rhythm of the day to falling three beats behind and spending the whole day trying to catch up. To explain this concept further, when we have faith that we are prepared and ready for the day, we go with the flow. We are not anticipating every move or trying to get ahead of the game. We accept the day for what it is and understand that we will deal with all its challenges and issues as they come. In this situation, it feels as if we are leaning back on the beat slightly. We feel relaxed and although it may not feel like we are achieving as much, we are actually keeping up with the day.

I am not here to tell you that you should lean forward or back on the beat of your day. Personally, I use a bit of both depending on the situation. What I have found however, that when I am leaning forward on the natural rhythm on the beat of my day, I have a tendency, whilst potentially being more productive, to have less self-discipline. This is to say, in these situations of high stress and anxiety, I am less inclined to exercise and more tempted to use less healthy options, such as alcohol, sugary, or fatty foods.

This, I feel, in the modern world is the great trade-off. We can find ourselves running around, leaning forward on our natural rhythm, increasing our stress levels with the expectation of achieving more. Whether you achieve more in these situations or not is very individual and personal. Whilst our natural instinct is to say that we do indeed achieve more in less time in a higher stress and anxious environment, I suggest this is not always the case. Much research and studies have been done in this area. Many have come to the conclusion that by focusing on the present, we may actually be more productive. We can also be more attuned to the modern world which is often manipulated to the advantage of others.

# Chapter 23

## Mindfulness

*"Mindfulness means paying attention in a particular way; on purpose, in the present moment, and non-judgmentally"*
Jon Kabat-Zinn

Companies and organizations spend billions of dollars preparing advertising campaigns that work to affect us in a subconscious manner. The way supermarkets set up the aisles, the way casinos don't have clocks and always have loud distracting noises, and the way product placement is used in television shows and commercials. We begin to build our interpretation of the environment in line with what others would like us to perceive. This induced perception does not sit right with us as individuals. It can create in a conflict and confusion. Even worse, we can fall prey to this kind of manipulation without even knowing.

Mindfulness can be used to counter-react the subconscious messages from organizations. It can also be used to build our own motivation, productivity, and performance. For example, studies have found[98] "Mindfulness to be associated with improved memory, motivation, and creativity," whilst others have found it to "Improve other work-related metrics, such as job satisfaction,"[99] "Emotional awareness,"[100] and "Social capital and workplace learning."[101] Recent studies have also reported "Links between mindfulness and improved workplace problem identification and coping skills,"[102] "Depression prevention and improved personal effectiveness,"[103] and "Mental resilience and psychosocial functioning in the workplace."[104]

We do not often think about using mindfulness in the workplace. Some may think, that mindfulness is something that you can only do whilst enjoying yoga, going for a walk, or being in nature. One study, designed to address fear in the workplace, found "Mindfulness to be associated with the capacity to make new meanings of familiar situations, think more clearly, and feel calmer, more empowered, and empathetic."[105]

Greats, such as Eckhart Tolle in his book The Power of Now, show us a way to better use mindfulness and "living in the present." Many like him, including myself, believe that by living in the now, and not always anticipating the immediate future, we are able to access an inner power that is not available to us when we are too focused about the next beat in the rhythm of our day.

Mindfulness meditation, is more specifically called insight meditation in Buddhist traditions, or vipassanna, which in Sanskrit means "to see clearly." Mindfulness refers to orienting one's self to the present moment. Definitions commonly emphasize maintaining an awareness of one's immediate experience, as opposed to being distracted by the past or future, or being engaged in the avoidance of one's experience. "Mindfulness meditation is a formal discipline that attempts to create greater awareness, and therefore foster greater insight in the practitioner."[106]

> *"Do not dwell in the past, do not dream of the future,*
> *concentrate the mind on the present moment"*
> *Buddha*

With higher levels of mindfulness, an individual can "Genuinely experience and express his/her emotions without over-engagement (e.g. entanglement) or under-engagement (e.g. avoidance) with them, which in turn enhances the individual's wellbeing. Emotions are simply accepted as they are, without any attempt to control, avoid or cling to them."[107]

By living in the now, we are in a much better position to enjoy the present. After all, we cannot change the past and the future depends on what we do today. We can only control the future to a point, and often, the more we try to control it, the less it goes our way. Contrary to what some people believe, by living in the now, we are often better prepared for the future than wasting our present preparing for it. This is especially true when the preparation is just thinking about the future as compared to a formal structure.

As we better understand our own emotions and how they change to different situations, we are more equipped to make better decisions in the future. By practicing the art of taking notice of the present, we become better at it. We become better at picking up the signs and signals in our environment. We notice things that will help us achieve our goals. Because we are not as concerned about the future, our stress levels are reduced. It is easier to remain positive and enjoy all the benefits that state has to offer. As described in more technical terms in the paper - Upward Spirals of Positive Emotions Counter Downward Spirals of Negativity, "Thus, people can intentionally increase their positivity ratios by learning to widen their attentional lens to encompass more of the pleasurable, interesting, and meaningful experiences in life, making the painful and dissatisfying ones smaller by comparison. In so doing, people learn to self-generate upward spirals that resonate within themselves and between themselves and others to increase their odds of flourishing."[108]

*"Mindfulness helps you go home to the present. And every time you go there and recognize a condition of happiness that you have, happiness comes"*
*Nhat Hanh*

# Chapter 24

## Meditation

*"To understand the immeasurable, the mind*
*must be extraordinarily quiet, still"*
*Jiddu Krishnamurti*

Meditation is another way that has been shown to access this inner power. Meditation has been shown to be one of the single most effective techniques to build productivity. I know for some this may seem counterintuitive. How could sitting on the floor cross-legged for half an hour possibly be a way to have a more productive day? I have practiced meditation for over 30 years. I have not practiced strictly or regularly and often it has been more the practice of mindfulness than serious meditation. Personally, I find it easier to clear the mind by incorporating mindfulness and exercise, whether it be it strenuous or non-strenuous. My experience is therefore a mix of mindfulness and meditation.

What I can say conclusively from this experience is that actively clearing the mind through meditation or mindfulness can be extremely effective to maximize productivity. This is achieved by allowing the mind to be clear of the rambling self-talk that we all know so well. This self-talk, we know, is 80% negative. This allows little chance to productively and proactively plan our day. I have found that as I calm the self-talk through mindfulness or meditation, my clear mind can resolve complex problems, both technical and logistical. After a session of mindfulness or meditation, I am often very clear on the precise steps I need to take to accomplish the goal. These goals may be normal day-to-day goals, or ones on a grander scale. Often after such sessions, I find myself quickly writing down my plan for the day or even long-term strategies.

Whilst there are people with far greater experience and knowledge on the workings of the human mind than I, I do understand the power of the practices comes from the increase in the ability of our subconscious mind to communicate with our conscious self. Our subconscious mind cannot communicate with us by conventional self-talk. It communicates with us through less tangible modes. It communicates through feelings, urges, impulses, and emotions. It has the ability to guide us in such a way that we can understand without actually hearing it. The more we can quiet our conscious mind and free ourselves from the distractions of the outside world, the easier it is to pick up on the thoughts, feelings, and emotions of our subconscious.

This has a very powerful effect on our ability to be efficient and effective in achieving our dreams, goals, and desires. We are also able to understand and articulate what it is we should be going after. This is something that is often overlooked or under appreciated. Our subconscious mind is much better equipped to know what is in our best interests and will be in line with our own personality traits and strengths. Our subconscious mind has access to all the historical data from our lives. It knows what has worked well for us, or not so well for us, in the past. It is acutely aware of what gives us deep emotional pain or satisfaction. Finally, it is not swayed by surface level pride or self-importance.

Conversely, when we do not trust and utilize our subconscious mind to help us discover our dreams and desires, we may find that we pursue activities that are not in harmony with our deeper self. We may find ourselves in situations where we do not feel contentment, fulfillment, or deep satisfaction. This can lead to all sorts of negative consequences. When we are not in line with our deeper self, this is where we experience roadblocks to efficiency and productivity, hindering our ability to achieve our goals. These roadblocks manifest themselves in a great variety of ways; they could be an addiction, smoking, drinking, gambling or drug, loss of motivation or even depression.

A famous study[109] proves a link between meditation and happiness. It began when the Dalai Lama invited Dr. Richard Davidson, a cognitive scientist at the University of Wisconsin-Madison, to interview monks about their mental and emotional lives. Davidson put 128 electrodes on the head of Matthieu Ricard, the French biochemist turned Buddhist monk.

When Ricard was asked to meditate on unconditional loving kindness (also known as compassion meditation, a particular strand of Buddhist meditation), the brain scans showed unusually high gamma waves.

The experiment also tested 8 monks with between 10,000 to 50,000 hours of meditative practice and a control group of non-meditating university students. Results were similar: "Not only did the monks produce 30 times more gamma waves than the control group, but much larger areas of their brains were activated during meditation, especially in the left prefrontal cortex, the part of the brain responsible for positive emotions."

In another study[110] of 139 working adults, half were trained in compassion meditation. "Results showed that this meditation practice produced increases over time in daily experiences of positive emotions, which, in turn, produced increases in a wide range of personal resources (e.g., increased mindfulness, purpose in life, social support and decreased illness symptoms)."

When we do not trust and utilize our subconscious mind in day-to-day and long-term planning, we are throwing away our most precious resource. We may find that we have not seen the obvious. We may find that we didn't think of a certain path or way of doing a task that we may have otherwise seen. We are more likely to have regrets and frustrations about how we performed our tasks or the ones that we did not do.

I strongly urge you to find a mindfulness or meditation practice that suits you and your lifestyle. Please do not try to follow an unsustainable practice. It is most beneficial to find something that works for you that you can integrate into your life for the long term. I urge you, when using these practices, to approach them with the attitude that you will gain benefit.

It can be very powerful to get into the habit of having a pen and paper available when you are performing these techniques. Get into the habit of writing something down, some insight or thought you had, during or after your session. This should not be overlooked. From my experience, there are two sides to the practice. The first is learning how to use mindfulness and meditation themselves. The next is to learn how to document and keep your insights, learnings, and takeaways. For some people, this could be recording their voice on their iPhone or using a notes application. For other people, like me, it may be making simple or sometimes complicated notes in a diary or workbook. Everyone has their own preferences. The key point is that in addition to learning how to meditate or use mindfulness, you must learn how to document the insights.

Sometimes insights are common sense, logical, and easy to integrate and use in your everyday life. Sometimes they are less tangible. Personally, I have found it is a valuable aim to capture as many insights as you can without getting hung up on where and how they may be used. Many insights or plans will end up never been used, but that is okay. Once you understand that at the time of documenting your insights, you may not know where and how they will be used, you are more likely to practice and perfect the technique in documenting them in the first place. Like a songwriter does not record all his songs, or a technician reviews different ways of fixing a problem before deciding on the ultimate course to take, you may come up with many insights and only use the ones that are relevant and will work in everyday life.

Life is a complex web of feelings, thoughts, and emotions. Relationships, responsibilities, and options all intertwine to produce this complex life full of challenges, choices, and decisions. By using only our conscious mind, we are ignoring the most powerful tool we have available to make sense of the vast array of choices and decisions we have to make every day. By partnering with our subconscious mind, and getting to know ourselves at a much deeper level, we are far better equipped to take on life's challenges, and overcome the obstacles that come our way. We get in touch with our inner knowledge. By building up our own resources and associating with others who also actively draw on their inner strengths, we create a team within ourselves and all around us. This group consciousness can achieve so much more than our single-minded, self-absorbed conscious mind ever would.

There is a lot of information available about meditation. There are also some great apps, like "Headspace" that can help you on your journey to build your mind through meditation.

# Chapter 25

## *The Self*

*"Drastic change creates an estrangement from self, and generates a need for a new birth of a new identity. And it perhaps depend on the way this need is satisfied whether the process of change runs smoothly or is attended with convolutions and explosions"*
*Eric Hoffer, The Temper of Our time*

## Self-Perceptions

In a highly connected world where we are always comparing ourselves with others, our self-esteem and a positive self-perception becomes increasingly important. I consider myself as being confident and with high self-esteem, yet I am still very concerned about how people perceive me. I can be affected easily if someone makes a negative comment about me. This is especially true if it is about something I am passionate about, like my work or hobbies. So although I consider myself as generally happy, this unfortunately can change very quickly.

Happiness is related to positive perceptions of our self in all life domains. Happy and content individuals have been found to be "More satisfied with their family life, romantic relationships, friends, health, education, jobs, leisure activities, and even their housing and transportation."[111] In a study of working adults, "Global happiness was found to be associated with intrinsically rewarding experiences, that is, activities that the individual wants to be doing for their own sake."[112] The authors of the study speculated that happy people may be able to perceive any activity, even routine, as intrinsically motivating, and therefore discover rewards even in ordinary, mundane events.

When in the zone, or in flow, people report feeling enraptured, as though in a different reality, lacking self-consciousness, and lacking a sense of the passage of time. We all love being in "the zone" or in "flow." We get it when we are enjoying our sports, hobbies, and other interests. Indeed, "Transient positive affect [happiness], is often accompanied by flow."[113] In a work situation, we all know that if we are engaged in the task, focused, and motivated, especially when we are happy to be there, the day passes quickly. When we are in the flow, or in the zone, we become happy and satisfied with the day's efforts and what we have achieved.

In my youth, a young man exploring the world, I worked as a lift operator at a ski resort. Myself and my close work colleagues and friends quickly found that if we approached work with a negative attitude, the day dragged on forever. Understanding this, we soon began to set ourselves challenges. We challenged ourselves to carve great on and off ramps in the snow. We aimed to make the loading process of the chairlift as quick and as friendly as possible and to make the skiing experience as warm and friendly as possible for the patrons. We learned that this sort of behavior, or attitude, not only gave us great satisfaction, but also made the day go quickly. Part of this was because we were keeping ourselves busy, but we were also being more appreciated. When we can find flow at work, this is when we succeed and enjoy our day. This is as true if you are a lift operator, cleaner, manager, or CEO. By acknowledging our situation and actively looking at ways to make it a happier and fulfilling environment, we can greatly impact how much we enjoy the day, and this in turn impacts the rest of our lives.

Across many studies, "People in a positive mood made faster and more efficient decisions in a personally relevant task,"[114] "Performed better on a clerical error checking task,"[115] and even "Considered the correct diagnosis of a disease earlier."[116] This is due to less anchoring, like where doctors cling to their first diagnosis, and are less likely to see other options. In this controlled experiment, doctors who were given a sweet (that he did not even eat, due to sugar affecting the experiment) were more flexible in their diagnosis. They could better explore options, and then ultimately come to a correct a diagnosis more often than those not given the treat!

The results of other studies also suggested more efficient processing. That is, participants placed in a positive mood were "Less likely to review information they had already seen, and were more likely to ignore information judged as unimportant."[117] In addition, the respondents high in happiness "Tended to eliminate alternatives that did not meet a minimum cut-off on important dimensions, a more efficient strategy. People in induced happy moods, also appear to persist longer at tasks in which perseverance is required."[118]

Happy people are generally more comfortable performing tasks. Their more frequent use of mental shortcuts "Allows them to allocate additional resources to secondary tasks, thus permitting them to use their time and resources more efficiently, and to perform well at complex problems."[119] Happy people are more flexible and creative. They use previous knowledge better and do not waste as much time on unnecessary tasks.

Think of your own experiences, when you were in the flow, when you found a task easier or more efficient. Were you in a positive or negative mood at the time? Instinctively, we know our self-esteem and self-perception is more accurate and more beneficial when we are in a happy and positive state of mind. This positive attitude helps to succeed, rather than the success producing the positive attitude. Whether at work, in our sports, or hobbies, such as playing music, if we are happy, it is easier to get into flow, or into "the zone." We love it because we are doing it well and enjoying the experience.

## Self-discrepancy

Self-discrepancy is the discrepancy between where you actually are in life and where you think you are or should be. Most of us live in some state of inner conflict. We have an image of the sort of person we are. This image is often slightly distorted from the actual reality of your life. Mindfulness and meditation really help in understanding what is really going on in our lives. Sometimes, this gap is very small and insignificant, and sometimes, it is extremely large.

Some studies, for example, asked people how often they exercise in one week or went to gym. The respondents who said they attended the gym three times a week were found to only go once or twice once their behavior was tracked. We often interpret our behaviors, whether it be our exercise, our diet, work performance, or social relationships as different to what is really going on. In addition, we often have a feeling of what we would like to be. I'm not talking about long-term goals, but more how we feel we should be behaving or acting. This gap between our actual and ideal or perceived reality can cause us conflict. This inner conflict may manifest itself in frustration, anxiety, or even depression. Various researchers have found evidence that "A felt discrepancy between the actual self and what one hopes to be can lead to disappointment and dissatisfaction."[120]

We do not wake up in the morning, jump out of bed, and ask ourselves "Is my actual reality equivalent to my perceived or ideal reality?" So this gap often goes unnoticed and lives somewhere deep in our subconscious. Meditation and mindfulness practices have been shown to narrow the gap. By performing these practices, we are better able to understand and accept our true reality, our true self. When we practice mindfulness or meditation, we begin to feel a calmness or serenity.

We put this feeling down to simply calming the mind. We should understand that there is more going on. That meditation and mindfulness is been proven to reduce the self-discrepancy. It was shown in a study of one hundred and twenty participants who took part in a mindfulness meditation course, "Before and after this, participants completed a self's questionnaire and the curiosity and exploration inventory. The findings confirm that mindfulness meditation can effectively reduce the gap between actual/ideal self attributes. In addition, curiosity is an influencing factor in making the largest changes in self-discrepancy after meditation."[121] Another study found "Meditation techniques aim to focus attention in a non-analytical way and attempt not to dwell on discursive, ruminating thought."[122]

Another way to look at self-discrepancy and the gap, is to think about what we notice in our own performance or the performance of others. Richard E. Boyatzis, who I referred to in the chapter on change, puts it this way, in his paper, An Overview of Intentional Change from a Complexity Perspective "All too often, people explore growth or development by focusing on the "gaps" or deficiencies. Organizational training programs and managers conducting annual reviews often make the same mistake. There is an assumption that we can "leave well enough alone" and get to the areas that need work"

How much better is life, when we know our strengths and weaknesses and think of ways we can use our strengths to get ahead? When running large telecommunications projects, I quickly learnt the engineer's strengths. Of course I was aware of their weaknesses, but for these large scale, projects to succeed, I needed to use their strengths.

Strengths are not always obvious and this is related to self-discrepancy. Take for example, engineers, who felt they are not really very valuable for the project, because of the level of complexity. Their skills may not really be up to the level required. When we sat down to review what value engineers could add to the project, we found although there skills may be slightly lacking, they were single and loved to travel. As many projects involved extensive travel this was a real advantage.

Many of the highly skilled engineers were married with children, so travel was problematic. These married engineers felt they were letting the team down due to their inability to travel. The less experienced ones, felt they were letting the team down due to lack of experience. A loose-loose situation soon became a win-win, when we developed a staging program, where the skilled engineers could prepare the systems to a point the less skilled ones could jump on a plane and install them.

This simple example, shows that we often have some inner conflict, about our own value. What we think we can contribute to the team. When we take the time to accept the situation and work with others for a resolution, instead of letting it bring us down, we can turn the whole situation around.

For me, many of these sort of breakthroughs, or resolutions to difficult issues came when meditating, or when I am doing sport, such as running or swimming, as the mind gets a chance to clear. The first step, is to talk to everyone involved and completely understand the situation, believe there is always a better way, then give yourself the opportunity to find the answer. This is especially true when you are the one experiencing self-discrepancy

## Simplicity and our true self

In a world with so many options and so many choices, it is easy to become overwhelmed. We are bombarded by marketing at supermarkets and on television, telling us what we need to live and how. If you are looking for efficiencies in your life, the same as with business, the key is simplicity. The true nature of life, in its essence, is simple - we make it far more complex than it really is. Be sure to take time out, whether through sport, meditation, or spiritual pursuits, to clear the mind and open yourself up to the simplicity of life.

> *"Many people take no care of their money till they come nearly to the end of it, and others do just the same with their time"*
> *Johann Wolfgang von Goethe*

I have spoken about the removal of roadblocks. This can be extremely powerful in the pursuit of peace and simplicity. The more things we remove from our life, the simpler it gets! We need to understand our true self. I'm not talking about our present self or life which is a product of many forces upon us, including our parents, our peers, and social expectations, to name just a few. I am talking about your true self. Think back to a time when you were energized, you were excited, and you felt like you could achieve anything. Think of how you felt. You may remember not being brought down by what others said or thought; you were free. At this point, you were closer to your true self than ever. This is what I mean by the true self.

By simplifying life, actively removing roadblocks, clearing the mind, and preparing your environment to be supportive and encouraging, you can experience your thoughts with more clarity and meaning. You're better in touch with emotions and this leads to better choices, behavior, and more focused action, enabling meaningful change easily and naturally. Always look for ways to simplify your life. This goes for your possessions, your commitments, and your state of mind. Another way to say this is do not over complicate your life. This we are very good at.

> *"Life is really simple, but we insist on making it complicated"*
> *Confucius.*

## Self Confidence

I talk a lot about self-confidence. The reason is simple: your ability to change greatly increases as your self-confidence grows. It is extremely important to know what you are good at, what your strengths are, and to acknowledge them. It is critical, like everything when we change, to write them down. The same goes for your accomplishments within your program of change, like reaching goals or completing tasks, or outside the program, like something you have completed or succeeded at. Learn to take credit for them; acknowledge your successes. You need to actively work on building your self-confidence.

The best way you can build your self-confidence is to follow a structure similar to this book. Use the tools and techniques to underpin this structure and really go for it. We build our self-confidence as we achieve what we have set out for ourselves. When we are clear on a vision, our dream, goals, and our plans and what it will take to reach them, we are ready for action. As we take action towards these things, we naturally build our self-confidence. As we celebrate the attainment of our goals, we build our self-confidence. As we look at ways to build in into the structure positive relationships, and utilise our signature strengths in everything we do, our tasks become easier and more enjoyable, hence building our self-confidence and self-esteem.

Building our self-confidence is all about taking action. It is not a destination; it is something we build on our way to another place. Whilst sometimes we need self-confidence in order to take specific action, there is always a preceding task that can lead us to the more difficult one. If you are not confident in talking to strangers, make more of an effort to talk to your friends. If you don't have many friends to talk to, build positive relationships with the people in your community or in your workplace. Look people in the eye, acknowledge what they are saying, ask questions, and be generally interested in the conversation. The more effort you put into building positive relationships, achieving your goals, and taking action in everyday life to learn and grow, the better your self-confidence will become., and the stronger your resilience.

This combination of confidence and resilience, allows you to see obstacles and hassle in your life as minor issues. When you encounter a roadblock, instead of seeing it as a major setback, you have the confidence and resilience to deal with it and move on. This is extremely powerful.

When I was at school. I was originally at a private school. It was a much protected environment. In those days the teachers could give students the strap, or on occasions even the cane! It was all about discipline. In year 9, I moved to a public technical school. Discipline was not really a concept they embraced. It was everyone for themselves. The playground, and often the class room was a war zone. Those without self-confidence and resilience were fair game to the bullies. My first year was hell. Without the experience in this environment, without the ability to change quickly to this new environment I was at risk. I was bullied and teased. In the protected environment of a private school, I had not developed resilience.

As it turned out, after a year of pain, I built my resilience and confidence. I began to understand my strengths. I was forced to change, I had to take action. I had to look people in the eye and make an effort to build relationships. These relationships became extremely important to me. We began to enjoy hobbies and interests together, I begun to enjoy life.

Whether you are being bullied at school or do not fit in with your work environment. If you have challenges in your personal life, with communication, self-confidence or resilience, you can do something about it. By following a structure, a process of change, by actively accepting your situation and deciding to do something about it, you can enjoy transformational change. You can take a situation that seems impossible and turn it around to your advantage.

You can build self-confidence, self-esteem and your resilience, not by tying to do it directly, but by building relationships. Also by building your interest and passion in what you are doing. By finding what you really love to do, and doing that. By sharing the experience with other like-minded people who also love doing what you do. This is the way we build our self-confidence.

# Chapter 26

## The Mind

*"Put your heart, mind, and soul into even your smallest acts. This is the secret of success"*
*Swami Sivananda*

## Neuroplasticity

In recent times, there has been much research on neuroplasticity and how we can take this concept to improve our lives. Neuroplasticity is defined as "The brain's ability to reorganize itself by forming new neural connections throughout life. Neuroplasticity allows the neurons (nerve cells) in the brain to compensate for injury and disease and to adjust their activities in response to new situations or to changes in their environment."[123]

Our brain physically changes in response to our thoughts, feelings, and our emotions. It can compensate for injury and disease, but also adjusts to new positive situations. Our physical brain can actually build itself to support our mission to succeed. We can build the neurons in our brain, we can even build the size of our hippocampus, depending on what we think about and how we use our brain.

The BBC news reported on a well-known study of London cab drivers coming out of the University College in London. They reported "Cab drivers' grey matter enlarges and adapts to help them store a detailed mental map of the city, according to research. Taxi drivers given brain scans by scientists at University College London had a larger hippocampus compared with other people. This is a part of the brain associated with navigation in birds and animals. There seems to be a definite relationship between the navigating they do as a taxi driver and the brain changes," said Dr. Eleanor Maguire, who led the research team.

We also know from other studies that we are able to train our minds to take certain neuronal pathways depending on the situation. It works a bit like learning to play the piano. At the beginning, a very simple piece of music is very difficult. The more we practice that piece of music, the better we become at. Our brains develop the neuronal pathways required in order to play the music. After much practice, we can play the music semi-automatically. I play guitar and find it hard to play in front of people, even though I do a lot of public speaking. It is not as much the nerves getting in front of people, but the risk of making a mistake. When I practice the same song over and over, eventually it just happens. At this point, I can look out to the audience and enjoy the moment more, because my mind just knows what to do with the guitar. There are so many situations in our lives where we develop this kind of neuronal pathway in order to complete a task.

As we begin to practice concepts, such as in this book or others that you may have adopted from elsewhere, like the first piece of music, it may seem a struggle in first. What we know scientifically is that the more often we practice these tools and techniques, new strategies, and thought patterns, the more natural they become. They become integrated into our lives and our minds through neuroplasticity. The structure of our mind actually changes to adjust to a new reality.

As this happens, our new reality becomes more natural and we unlearn some of our old bad habits. Our perception of our world and our reality is through the workings of our internal mind. So as we begin to adjust our minds, we are in fact adjusting our reality. When we take on a mindset of success and abundance, a mindset where we discover expanding possibilities and identify new opportunities, our mind naturally adjusts to support us in our mission.

This is been proven through science. In one study on the life-long stability of neurons, we learn "Neuronal connections in the adult brain are malleable to experience."[124] Such plasticity may involve a whole host of structural changes to the brain, including changes in the strength of synaptic connections and the proliferation and arborization (a fine branching structure at the end of a nerve fiber) of neurons, which has been documented in the brains of adults exposed to a variety of enriching learning experiences.

Neuroplastic changes have been shown to result from a diverse range of physical and mental forms of training. Across these varied activities, a commonality can be gleaned: "Recurrent practice of novel responses and repeated experiences that 'stretch' one beyond his or her previously established limits are associated with the development of potentiated synaptic connections and new neural growth."[125]

Whether it be through meditation, exercises to build positivity, gratitude, or any number of techniques, we can build our minds, just as we can build our bodies at the gym. According to one researcher, "The short-term cognitive and attentional effects of positive emotions are what lead to gradual, long-term growth."[126]

So the more we build up our positive emotions, the more we look for the good in situations, the more we challenge ourselves and strive towards our purpose, our meaning and what we really want in life, the more we are building our minds to support us in our mission. This is the very foundation of the upward spiral to success. This is how we build, not only external resources through our success, but our internal resources; our mental ability to achieve what is most important to us.

*"All the resources we need are in our mind"*
*Theodore Roosevelt*

## Mirror Neurons

The positive emotions that we share with other people affect them in many ways, including using our mirror neurons. When we project positivity and happiness, even a smile, the other person is naturally inclined to feel those emotions and vice versa.

Mirror neurons are one of the most important discoveries in the last decade of neuroscience. These are physical neurons in our brains. They are a variety of visuo-spatial neurons which indicate fundamentals about human social interaction. A study on this concludes, "Essentially, mirror neurons respond to actions that we observe in others. The interesting part is that mirror neurons fire in the same way when we actually recreate that action ourselves."[127] This is why happiness and positivity is contagious, as with negativity.

The more we build positivity and happiness in our lives, the easier we are able to experience these emotions in the future. This has been proven in research on neuroplasticity. Our brains actually create new neurological pathways to allow us to automatically experience this positivity and happiness under certain conditions. The more we experience these emotions, the more we can share them with other people by way of activating their mirror neurons. When they are happy and positive, that reflects back to us in a positive way.

If you stand in front of someone and they give you a big smile, you generally will smile also, as your mirror neurons light up, just the same as when you stand in front of someone who is yawning. The smile or the yawn that the other person is projecting is interpreted by your mind, as if you are also experiencing that smile of a yawn. This is why it is so important to build positive relationships. This is why it is so important to ensure you are in a positive environments where people share the same drive and passion as yourself.

# Chapter 27

## Silence the Noise

*"We need to find God, and he cannot be found in noise and restlessness. God is the friend of silence. See how nature - trees, flowers, grass- grows in silence; see the stars, the moon and the sun, how they move in silence. We need silence to be able to touch souls"*
*Mother Teresa*

One of the best ways to free your mind for happiness and success is to silence the noise. Noise can take away our peace and tranquility. It gets in our way of relating to our higher power, our inner, or outer strength. Or in the words of Mother Teresa "God is the friend of silence." The noise can be both internal and external. By silencing the noise, our minds are more open and free to discover things that will help us to achieve our goals and our ambitions. In this section, we identify and look at ways to reduce the noise.

Mindfulness and mediation are practices to clear the mind. Reducing the noise is an ongoing strategy that gives our mind the time and space to be creative, motivated, and engaged without the distractions of modern life. Some of the noise we experience is very personnel. We may not be able to, or want, to eliminate all the noise, but we should at least take time to understand where it is coming from and what we can do about it. The following are only suggestions of areas you may want to address. Everyone has their own likes and dislikes. Please accept the following as a guide and not my recommendations. Find the areas you are willing and able to reduce the noise in. Discover what works for you.

**Ways to reduce the external noise**
- Reduce time consuming news
- Cut the commercials
- Let stocks and other prices go up and down
- Manage your time on social media
- Limit time in non-relevant conversations
- Cut down screen time by 10%
- Create silence
- Ask if it is relevant or timely?

**Ways to reduce the Internal Noise**
- Meditation and Mindfulness
- Notice just 10 breaths.
- Exercise
- Notice the noise
- Keep the worry in proportion to the reality
- Do not be afraid every day, to stop something happening every thousand days
- Do not equate worrying with being loving or responsible

# Chapter 28

## External noise

*"Silence is a true friend who never betrays"*
*Confucius*

Much of the noise in our environment does not serve us. We are creatures of habit and the only way to really know if we need, or really want, something in our lives, especially when it comes to noise, is to experiment with reducing it. The reason is simple. We get very accustomed to our environment. We get so accustomed to the sights, the sounds, and even the people in our life we barely notice them. Please make an effort to reduce the noise in your environment that does not serve you. Have fun with this exercise and experiment. You may be surprised what happens when you free your environment up from some of the noise. Like cleaning your house or office, the cleanliness brings clarity and order. We can also clean our audible world. The effect is less tangible because you cannot see it. The benefits, however, can be even more valuable.

### The news

We intently watch the news in the evening. This, in itself, is not a massive problem. That said, we have an obsession to follow stories and we want the latest update immediately. This often means we watch the news twice in one day, and read updates on the internet, or on our smart phones. I do not suggest that you need to cut the news from your life. When reducing the external noise, it can be useful to attempt reducing it by 20%, for example. If you make a conscious effort to understand how much time you are spending absorbing news, you can then compare that with what you can do about that news, or how helpful it is for you to achieve your goals. Once you better understand your consumption and the reason for it, you may find it easier to reduce your intake.

It is estimated that some 15% to 20% of the news we digest is the weather. We all know how often the weather predictions can be wrong. Some say they are wrong more often than they are right. Is it really worth our valuable time to listen to unreliable predictions on the weather? We also need to ask ourselves whether listening to the weather on a weeknight, for example, makes any difference to the actions we take the next day.

Please review your consumption of news. Look at the most effective and efficient ways you can receive the news. Should you receive it on-line, on your phone, or on the television? Can you listen to the radio on the way to work? Again, I am not suggesting you need to eliminate the news, just make a conscious effort to ensure that you are consuming it in the most effective, efficient, and enjoyable way.

## Television commercials

Television commercials make up nearly one third of a one hour show. I do appreciate the importance of advertising to allow us free content and fully support that we should get behind companies who are willing to provide us this content. We do, however, need to be very aware of the time we spend watching television commercials. With all the modern technology available and alternate viewing options, there is little reason why we should dedicate one third of our viewing time to watching advertising. This time is a complete waste in regards to our success. Make a conscious effort to reduce the time you watch television advertising. If you do not, or cannot eliminate it, at least make an effort to reduce it by some 20% to 50%.

## Stock prices

Monitoring of stock prices, and other commodities, seems to be a full-time occupation for some people. If you are a day trader, this of course is common sense. If you are not actively buying or selling stock, this can be a complete waste of time. For some people, like gambling, participating in this task can be addictive. If this is the case for you, I suggest you take steps to recognize your situation and manage it. This could be as simple as taking short cuts or alerts off your computer or smart phone. Ask yourself whether monitoring the stock prices is really benefiting your strive for happiness and success.

## Social media

There are whole books dedicated to social media. The pros and cons of social media have been documented, discussed, and debated for many years. Of course social media has a place in our modern world. Unfortunately, it is very effective in sidetracking us from our purpose. We all know the feeling, when we were are completing a task that we may not be completely passionate about, or hit a little roadblock, about the temptation to check our Facebook or other social media account. For many people, it is an addiction. You do not need to look at Facebook for long to know the people who are on it all the time. It is worth asking yourself whether all this time on social media is really propelling you to what is most important in your life. I am not suggesting cutting it out, just limiting it, or at least managing it.

In the workplace, I have seen reports from IT departments about users who not only have their social media accounts open, but are active on them for four hours a day! This may seem excessive, but I would like to issue you a challenge. For one day, or a full week, whichever you can handle, write down every single time you are on social media. This includes even a quick look at your Facebook page or a quick Tweet. Even though reading a short tweet that is only five seconds long seems insignificant, the research tells us that the time to get back into the task we were doing previously is a lot longer than we think.

A useful strategy is to simply plan out allocated times each day to use social media. I discuss in many parts of this book the importance of social interactions. So actively managing how you incorporate social media into your life can be very useful. If you take the train or bus to work, there is plenty of time to stay connected. Over breakfast, or in the evening, rather than watching TV, or during those television commercials or the weather, you can find time. Even a quick check over your coffee break or lunch break is fine. If you are serious about happiness and success, there should be no reason to use otherwise productive time during your day on social media.

## Other people

So here is my big contradiction. Social relationships are extremely important, yet sometimes we need to limit the chatter. If there is someone at your work, or social group, who talks way too much, please understand you do not need to listen to them all the time. We all know who they are; the friend or work colleague who just can't stop talking. Often these conversations are very one-sided, usually about them, or negative gossip about other people. How are you meant to succeed in work and life if you give these people your time? Of course, the friend or co-worker may be a really great person. I suggest a simple strategy is to increase engagement with this person, whilst reducing the time spent listening to them. Next time this friend or co-worker comes over for a long chat, get on the front foot. Ask them something about their life. Ask them about their kids, family, or others they were talking about last time. Use names whenever possible. Be as engaged and interested in the conversation as you can. Rather than just standing there listening to them, be the most interested and engaged person they have spoken to all day. Now, the trick. At the very beginning of the conversation, or alternatively after only a few minutes, make some comment such as "I would really like to hear about your aunt Betty, but I only have a few minutes." Or you could say "Great to see you. I only have a few minutes, but whatever happened with your son's soccer team?" You can be creative and make up your own. The main points is that if you actively engage for a very short time, yet plan your escape route so the conversation takes up the minimal amount of time, your friend or co-worker will not think you are rude. They will believe you are more interested in them now than you ever were previously. Please limit the time spent listening to people when there is no meaningful engagement or purpose in the conversation.

## Television and other screen time

I spoke about television commercials, now the elephant in the room; television and other screen time. Over my life, I have spent at least 10 years without a television. Now, with three children, 10 and under, I love watching television. The time I did not have a television, I did not miss it. We would read books, play games, talk, etc. Now, after a long day of working and dealing with kids, sitting down to a couple of hours of mindless TV is most enjoyable. I could quote many studies that state the absurd amounts of screen time the average adult indulges in every day. Everyone is different and uses it for their own purpose, so I'm not here to preach the sins of the television or surfing the net. I will suggest however, that it can be extremely beneficial to limit your screen time. The easiest way, of course, is to just get out more. Join a local art class, social group, or sports club. Meet up with friends, go for a walk, or just get out of the house.

An easier strategy, one to use when you are going to be at home, is to simply push back the time you begin watching. Instead of automatically turning on the television when you get home or after dinner, read the newspaper, magazine, or a good book for 30 minutes. Even aiming only to read 10 minutes helps. Put the remote control in the other room and start reading. You may find by this simple exercise that you end up reading for a lot longer than you originally thought. Of course, instead of reading, you could play a game, talk, play guitar, or whatever suits you. The point is to understand how much time you spend watching television and aim to reduce it, even if by only 10%. You may find that 10% you spend doing something else gives you much satisfaction and enjoyment. It may even open up opportunities that will positively affect your chances of happiness and success.

## Music, video games, television, and other background noise

It can be extremely powerful to spend time in a silent home or other environment. Sometimes, by simply turning the radio, the CD, iPod, or the television off, we can enjoy a fundamental shift in our mental state of mind. The silence brings us clarity and allows us to solve problems, sometimes unconsciously, that we would not have been able to do while being bombarded by external noise.

## Is it relevant or timely?

So much of the noise in our lives is not relevant or timely. No matter if it is surfing the Internet, watching television or reading newspapers. If there is not a reason to consume it, why should we bother? If we are consuming the information just for pleasure or relaxation, as long as we understand this, it is okay. The problem begins when we are consuming information that may be interesting, but it is not relevant to us at this time. We may feel because it's interesting, we should read it, watch it, or listen to it. But if this information is not required by us for another six months, we are most likely going to forget it. So why bother with it in the first place?

## Chapter 29

# Internal Noise

*"To know yourself as the Being underneath the thinker,
the stillness underneath the mental noise, the love and joy
underneath the pain, is freedom, salvation, enlightenment"*
*Eckhart Tolle*

The internal noise, the self-talk, can be much more challenging to silence than the outside noise. You have already read the section on mindfulness and meditation. These two techniques have been proven to be some of the most effective techniques to reduce the inner noise. It is undeniable that after practicing meditation and/or mindfulness, you experience or are closer to a state of clarity and serenity. The effects of meditation are so powerful. If you are having problems quietening the inner voice, you should seriously consider taking up one of the many meditation practices. This could be a very strict and regular practice or as simple as taking notice of your breathing.

## Taking notice of your breathing

An extremely quick, easy, and effective way to quiet your mind is to stop what you're doing and notice your next 10 breaths. Try not to think about anything else, but breathing in and exhaling. Take special care to notice the gap between the exhale and the inhale. Meditation practitioners have known the power of noticing this gap for thousands of years. If you have the discipline, by practicing this short technique many times throughout the day, you will enjoy less internal chatter and more clarity with minimal effort.

# Exercise

One of the best ways to quiet a stressed out mind is to exercise. This exercise should not be confused with the exercise you do to maintain a fit and healthy body. Of course they can be one and the same, but in this section, we are talking about the mind. By committing to doing a short 15 minutes of exercise each day, you can enjoy more control of your inner mind. The 15 minutes does not need to be completed in leotards, shorts, or running shoes. By simply getting up from your desk and taking a 15 minute walk in the sunshine, or the rain for that matter (which I personally find provides more benefit), gives your mind a chance for clarity. If during that exercise, you can try some mindfulness practices, such as noticing your breath, the trees you walk past, or simply enjoy the smells, sights, and sounds, you will gain maximum advantage from that activity.

# Notice the noise

By simply identifying the noise in your head, your self-talk, you are in a lot better position to manage it. You may take a mental note of what it is saying and physically write that down on paper or on a word document. The important thing is to actively notice the noise. Once you know what the noise is, you can challenge or question it. By simply asking yourself; is this internal chatter conducive to my success, you are reducing the power it has on you.

# Manage the Noise

Shawn Achor, in his book, Before Happiness, gives three very useful techniques to quiet the internal worry. I elaborate with my own thoughts about these techniques below.

**1. Keep the worry in proportion to the reality.** Are you thinking over and over again about something that does not really affect your reality? Is the time and mental energy you are spending on this thought in proportion to its effects in your real world?

**2. Do not fear every day, to stop something happening every thousand days.** I think in his book, he says "Do not fear every day, to stop something happening every 10,000 days." The point is the same. We often think, over and over again, about situations, circumstances, or possibilities that we think we need to negate, or find solutions for. Often these fears are unfounded, with a minimum possibility of them ever happening. Even if they do happen, often the result or outcome of the situation is minimal, or can be dealt with at the time without previous planning. So when you're worrying about something over and over in your mind, simply ask the question; Is this a fear that I should really waste my mental time and energy on? If the fear is real, you should not spend your time just thinking about it. You should write down the fear, the challenge, or concern you have. You should then write the probability that it may happen, the risk, or outcome if it happens, and what you can do about. By writing these things down, they will move out of your head and onto the paper. They will become clearer and easier to understand.

   **3. Do not equate worrying with being loving or responsible**. Too often, we worry about things because we think this is the loving or responsible thing to do. Concerns and situations go around and around in our mind. We feel by thinking about them, it means we are a better person; that we care about somebody or something and that thinking about the situation somehow makes it better. Just like the point above, if we are worrying about something that will affect someone we love or are responsible for, we should actively manage that situation by writing down the strategy to overcome it. By lying awake for hours at night letting the problem or concern go around and around in our minds is helping no one.

## Summary

   Whether it be internal or external noise, the more we reduce it, the better off we are. As you can see, there are many different sources of this noise. This means we don't necessarily have to cut out any one thing completely. We should simply aim to reduce the overall noise the best we can. If you want to reach into your subconscious knowledge base and find solutions to your most pressing problems, you should limit the noise. If you want to give your mind the space to come up with original and creative ways of dealing with your day-to-day situations and longer term goals, you should quieten the noise. The more silent our environment, the more in touch we are with our intuition and our gut feelings. We find peace and serenity through a calm mind.

# Chapter 30

## The Joy of Stress

*"The key to surviving and thriving on stress is control not avoidance"*
*Dr. Peter G Hansen*

There is a great book by Dr. Peter G Hansen called The Joy of Stress. In his book, Dr. Hansen explains how a great percentage of his patients experienced sickness or illness due to stress, and of all the illness and accidents, stress accounts for three quarters of all time lost from work.

Dr. Hansen says, "Strive to maximize success, by investing your energy and time in all four quadrants of your life – financial sufficiency, personal happiness, sound health, and respect on-the-job." He makes the point that too little stress can be as dangerous as too much stress. Dr. Hansen's book is all about making active choices. He says, "The reality is that good choices are extremely easy and fun, while it is the bad ones that are complicated and deadly." "The key to surviving and thriving on stress" he says, "is control not avoidance."

I refer to Dr. Hanson and his book as it is a great example of using tools and techniques in your current job and life to increase your health and well-being. He does not suggest that you find an easier job with less stress, or a harder job with more stress that makes the day go quicker. The answer is using a positive mental attitude to actively control your situation for a better outcome.

If we want to reduce the adverse effect of stress in our lives, instead of running from it, we should focus on it. Too many stress management classes and training programs focus on the negative effects of stress. They tell us we should not stress and give us tools and techniques to reduce our stress in the workplace and in our social lives. There is another side to this coin, an alternate perspective on stress. If we can find the meaning in our stress and understand where it comes from, we are in a better position to deal with it.

When I was managing large projects, my stress levels did get very high. This was especially the case as we were working on production systems or putting a system into production. Due to this, I do understand it is easier to say "do not stress" than to actually make it happen. I did find, as I accepted the situation for what it was, especially when things went bad, the stress level lowered. Of course, sometimes that situation meant accepting I may not get any sleep that night and have some tense conversations in the morning. Here, I found, was the trick. I speak about thinking positive, however, for me to reduce the level of stress, I found I needed to accept the negative, the worst case scenario. Once I could accept what could go wrong and how bad things could get, I could focus on the positive. How could we resolve the issue as quickly as possible? Once I had accepted the worst, I was more relaxed and committed (because I knew how bad it could get) to find a resolution.

Our brains are trained to give more power to negative thoughts. So when our situation becomes stressful, it is normally because we are putting too much emphasis on the negative consequences or part of the situation. If we take time to examine the situation we are in, and what the risks and potential rewards are, we can better understand our situation. Once we better understand the situation, we are in a better position to understand our stress. Instead of letting the stress run our lives, promote poor eating, or increased substance abuse, with the right mental attitude, we can use that same stress to motivate us and inspire us.

Shawn Achor, along with another researcher, used a three-minute video to teach managers at financial services firm UBS how to view stress as enhancing rather than debilitating. Six weeks later, that group had better productivity as well as a 23% drop in fatigue-related health problems compared with a group that saw a video portraying stress as traumatic.

Accepting stress as a natural part of life and a challenge that we all deal with, is so important. Once we understand that stress also has a positive side and that it is not always detrimental to our health and our well-being, we can better use it to achieve success and happiness. Once we can look at the stress for what it is and understand what is causing that stress, we are better able to handle the situation. We can take the emotion away from the stress and look at ways to use it to our advantage. It is much better to manage your approach to stress than to fall victim to it.

This does not mean we need to always strive for stress. Stress as a normal part of high performance. But there are limits and <u>recovery</u> is key. There is a bell curve relationship that happens. Two little stress is not good, neither is too much stress. There is a sweet spot.

The Yerkes-Dodson Law suggests that there is a relationship between performance and arousal. Increased arousal can help improve performance, but only up to a certain point. At the point when arousal becomes excessive, performance diminishes. The better we can understand the stressful situation we are in, and make sure it has not gone too far; that it is not asking too much from us, the better we can deal with it and even benefit from it.

*"Some executives thrive under pressure. Others wilt. Is the reason all in their heads? Hardly. Sustained high achievement demands physical and emotional strength as well as a sharp intellect. To bring mind, body, and spirit to peak condition, executives need to learn what world-class athletes already know: recovering energy is as important as expending it."*
*Jim Loehr and Tony Schwartzn- The Making of a Corporate Athlete*

The Yerkes-Dosan Law tells us there are four stages, in a pyramid of success. Well-being is its foundation. Above that rests emotional health, then mental capacity, and at the top, a sense of purpose. The Ideal performance state, peak performance under pressure, is achieved when all levels are working together. All these stages are joined together with rituals. Rituals that make us strong and let us achieve what we need to, in order to reach the next state. Rituals that help to offset feelings of stress and restore positive energy.

# Chapter 31

## Post-Materialism

*"It is the preoccupation with possessions, more than anything else that prevents us from living freely and nobly"*
*Bertrand Russell*

In a post-financial crisis world, many people are starting to question some of the old world ideals. Where previously the world was run by materialism and commercialism, a new post-materialism world is developing. Many people are now starting to understand that autonomy, self-expression, meaning, and purpose are so much more important than wealth and material goods. We have seen our parents, friends, and family lose all that they have worked for. The loss of wealth has been through pyramid schemes, bad investments, poor choices, or bad advice. The loss of possessions has been through fire, theft, or simply the inability to store and use all the products we have purchased over the years.

We begin to understand how fragile or world really is. Not just our possessions, but life itself. The more we understand how precious and fragile this life we have really is, the better we are able to make decisions about how we treat ourselves, our friends and our money.

I wrote a song back in 2002, which although very simple, has a special place in my heart. I think about it when I start to lose touch with what is really important.

*For the musicians among you, it is played using a finger picking progression, G, C, D, C. Repeating the D cord near the end over <u>more</u> and also <u>pray.</u>*

*FRAGILE*
*(G) Well I know my life is (C) fragile, (D) so fragile (C) indeed,*
*It's fine lines and crazy times, I know I don't*
*want to leave, (extra bar on the C)*
*But if I had to go tomorrow, I'd had a really good time,*
*Short it would have been and places I haven't seen, but*
*at least I know it mine (extra bar on the C)*

*So let's just pray for today and ask the sky above*
*For one more day like today and many more.......*
*to come (extra bar on the C)*
*Well yes life is fragile, so fragile indeed,*
*We don't know about tomorrow, we just pray......*
*that it will come. (extra bar on the C)*
Michael Hunt 2002

Yes life is fragile, so fragile indeed. So why should we waste a single moment on obtaining goods that are not directly required to achieve our prime purpose? Why should we spend time and money on things that we, deep down, know will not have a direct positive impact in our lives?

"Materialism is the placing of a relatively high value on the possession of wealth and material goods."[128] "Post-materialism is the transformation of individual values from materialist, physical and economic to new individual values of autonomy and self-expression."[129] The post-materialism ideal, can be viewed in line with the famous Maslow's Hierarchy of Needs that tells us once we have our basic needs met, we then look for love, belonging, and self-esteem to reach self-actualization. Maslow suggested that we first must meet the most basic requirements of life; Air, water, food, clothing and shelter. We must then insure our safety, first physical, away from the war, natural disaster, violence or abuse, plus taking care of basic health and well-being requirements, and then our emotional and financial security, such things as job security, adequately insured and other basic safety nets. Once we have satisfied these basic needs, Maslow suggests the next foundation is love and belonging; things such as friendship, intimacy, and family. According to Maslow, humans need to feel a sense of belonging and acceptance among their social groups. Self-esteem presents the typical human desire to be accepted and valued by others. The pinnacle of life, Maslow states. "What a man can be, he must be,"[130] Maslow once said. In his later years, Maslow explored a further dimension of needs - self transcendence, which looks at a power higher than oneself, a more spiritual realm.

What I find is the most interesting part of Maslow's Hierarchy of Needs is the complete absence of materialistic possessions outside those that provide us with our basic necessities of life. This belief, or finding, by Maslow is not unique. It is being shown in numerous studies all around the world that once a person's basic needs are met, increased wealth and materialist possessions provide a person only slightly more happiness.

Research on the relative happiness of wealthy and poor people makes it clear that "Financial success beyond what is necessary for sufficient food, shelter, and clothing has a relatively small effect on well-being."[131] Moreover, researchers routinely find that "Individuals who focus on the acquisition of material objects exhibit reduced life satisfaction."[132] They experience "Diminished levels of happiness,"[133] and "Higher levels of depressive symptoms."[134] The research is clear. By chasing after satisfaction through materialism, we are destined to fail in our search. Studies have also shown that, "Materialistic people also tend to be less satisfied with other aspects of their lives such as their standards of living, their family lives, and the amounts of fun and enjoyment they experience."[135] "Similar associations have been documented in samples of individuals rich and poor, and young and old, from around the world."[136]

*"Individually, people are finding that a simpler lifestyle provides greater satisfaction than relentless pursuit of materialism"*
*Laurence Rockefeller*

So whilst the pursuit of money and goods to look after ourselves and our family is important, it does seem that once we reach a certain level, it becomes less important. The problem is when we get so obsessed in making money and collecting materialistic possessions that it gets in the way of building our relationships and own personal experiences. The pursuit of wealth and possessions as an end unto itself has been shown to be "Associated with lower levels of well-being, lower life satisfaction and happiness, more symptoms of depression and anxiety, more physical problems such as headaches, and a variety of mental disorders."[137] Contrary to what we may immediately think, materialism has been shown to have "A negative association with nearly every quality of life measure studied to date."[138]

With this information in mind, it is easier to see why the post-materialistic movement is becoming a reality. That said, we are all guilty of wanting a new car, a better home, and more possessions. I do not suggest that anyone should get rid of all their possessions and live a life of scarcity. I do suggest, however, that it is worthwhile to evaluate your wants and needs regarding physical possessions with an open mind. It can be worthwhile to weigh up the advantages of additional possessions against the time and effort it takes to earn the funds to purchase them. It is also worthwhile, when you are spending your money, to think of the benefits you will receive from materialistic possessions as compared to experiences, adventures, and the like. We now know how important it is to build social capital, to get out and enjoy life with other people, and to do what you love. Even if you are doing a sport or a hobby that is cheap or free, such as surfing, hiking, etc., you still often need to spend money to get there, for equipment, and anything else that makes it an enjoyable day.

It truly is a balancing act between experiences and possessions, plus the time and effort to achieve the resources required. Within our families, research shows that "Parenting styles that fail to satisfy children's needs may lead to higher materialism in children."[139] One study found that "Young adults raised in families in which the parents were divorced or separated were more materialistic and exhibited higher levels of compulsive consumption than did those who were raised in intact families."[140]

The more we understand about materialism, the more we understand its true nature. Depending on the way we were brought up and our own personal perspective on life, we become more or less materialistic.

"Cross-cultural work has shown that large-scale economic factors also influence materialism. People living in poorer countries were more materialistic than those living in richer countries, generations raised in poor economic times are more materialistic than those raised in richer times, and national recessions tend to result in increased materialism."[141] Poor economic conditions, therefore, can "Cause feelings of insecurity for which people sometimes compensate by turning to materialistic pursuits."[142] These findings support why, now as we become richer and more affluent, we may start to be less materialistic and look to more personal qualities for satisfaction and meaning.

That said, although we are more affluent, we spend more time watching television or on the internet where advertising is rampant. Television is an arena for exposure for incessant materialistic messages. Accordingly, "Materialism has been associated with a high amount of television watching across numerous cultures. Television reveals a discrepancy between people's own lives and cultural ideals, and these unrealistic media images reduce life satisfaction."[143]

Everyone must find their own balance. We need to put up our own filter to discern what we really need and what we have been told we need. We need to question our purchases and be clear if we are getting value for money. Is this purchase satisfying a real need or are we using it to stroke our ego or provide retail therapy? By becoming increasingly aware of our true purpose in life, our deepest dreams and desires, and questioning whether our purchases are in line with this, we can make better decisions. By ensuring our purchasing decisions are in line with our goals, we can decrease expenditure on what is not important and utilize those resources to help us succeed in reaching our goals.

# Chapter 32

# Product vs. Experience

*"The only source of knowledge is experience"*
*Albert Einstein*

Once we understand what we don't need to buy in life the question then becomes; what should we spend our money on? Do experiences make people happier than material possessions? In two surveys, respondents from various demographic groups indicated that "Experiential purchases--those made with the primary intention of acquiring a life experience--made them happier than material purchases. In a follow-up laboratory experiment, participants experienced more positive feelings after pondering an experiential purchase than after pondering a material purchase."[144]

In another study, respondents asked to evaluate an experiential purchase indicated that it made them happier than did those asked to evaluate a material purchase. Respondents also indicated that experiential purchases were better financial investments than material purchases. Participants indicated that, "Compared with material purchases, experiential purchases made them happier, contributed more to their happiness in life, and represented money better spent. They were also less inclined to say that the money spent on experiences could have been better spent elsewhere than the money spent on material possessions."[145]

I have to admit I am bias in this area. I have traveled extensively. I have lived abroad and taken the time to experience other counties and cultures. This has given me, not only great pleasure, but a different perspective on my life in Australia. I spent 5 years sharing my time between the ski fields of North America, and a coastal rural town, on a perfect right hand surf break, in Oaxaca, far south Mexico. Here, with my brother, we built, and still have a rustic beach house. The only house on the beach.

Whilst at the time, in my early 20's this may have seemed like a waste of time, from a financial and career perspective, it gave me great insights. These lessons and experiences stayed with me through my corporate career, and now into my career as a life coach and trainer. The experience, of meeting people, both very rich and very poor helped me appreciate different perspectives on life. I saw people at all socio economic levels, struggle with very similar life issues. This experience was invaluable. I could not have gained such pleasures, nor experiences by buying a new car or LED TV.

This time has lead me to always want to experience the most out of life. After I meet my wife, we planned for more than 4 years, then took a year sabbatical. We traveled extensively around the world for a year. We bought an around the world ticket, and enjoyed 33 separate flights to all sorts of places in Africa, Europe, North and South America and Asia. We were backpacking and camped in most places. An interesting fact, is that we spent less money that year, than we had spent any of the four years prior, living in Australia, although we did not earn any money either!

So often, we are scared to take the big step. To try an experience that is new. Whether it is a year sabbatical, or a weekend away. We get caught up in life's roles and responsibilities. We find all sorts of reasons why not to go bungee jumping, camping, ski diving, snorkeling, canoeing etc. There is always a valid reason why not to do anything, when you really think about it.

Deciding to take the chance and commit to an experience, creates a snow ball effect. After spending those 5 years away when I was young, I understood what was possible. I then took the year sabbatical and traveled the globe. More recently, with my wife and children, we have traveled extensively and even spent 2 years skiing, biking and hiking in Whistler Canada. Originally the trip was to be one year, but we stayed an extra year because it was just so much fun!

I am not here to tell you how great my life is. I, like everyone else have had my share of challenges and issues. Among this, I still spent 20 year working in the corporate world, commuting into the city every day. I worked long hours and had to deal with a lot more problems than anyone should have to face. Unrealistic expectations from managers, and employees who think they have more problems than myself. As I mentioned earlier, I was bullied at school, also my parents separated when

I was in my early teens. Unfortunately most of us have issues in our life, no matter where we live, or how much money we have. It is what we do with what we have, that really counts.

The benefit from all my experience, traveling and learning about all different environments, was that I could keep my situation in perspective. I could see my situation for what it was. I could think back to people I had meet, who would die to be in the position I was in, no matter how stressful it was. I could understand some of the challenges other people were in, as the problems people face are common around the globe. I could, when times became really tough, think back when I was traveling and enjoying myself, and realise that life really was not that bad after all. Most of all, I felt I had something to offer, to my employees. Not just in knowledge, but more in perspective. To help them appreciate what they had. That all was not really as bad as they thought.

Experiences really are so much more valuable than products. We not only enjoy them, but we take the feeling, the excitement and the knowledge with us. We hold onto it, we can recall it and tell the story, and more importantly we know we have done it. We are better able to change our perspective on other life events. We remember how and why we decided to do it, and this makes it easier to do it again. It really is the snow ball effect.

It all makes sense really. When we enjoy an experience, it is unique to us. We take it on and complete it in our own special way. We perceive the experience very personally. We also enjoy looking forward to experiences. We can enjoy the lead up, share the excitement with friends, and use it to get through difficult days. We then think back to the experience usually in a very positive way. In fact, we often think back to the experience more positively than we actually experienced it at the time. This is because we can focus on what we enjoyed and forget any hardships getting to or during the experience. We also get bored of our possessions such as a new car, new phone, or other toys quickly. They become a normal part of our existence. We buy something to make us happy and very soon, we are looking for the next good thing to purchase. I have moved house and even country a few times in my life. So often, as I reduce my possessions so I do not need move them or pay for storage, I think back to when I paid good money for them. Often I tell myself, I could have easily lived without that item. Even worse is when I keep it because I spent good money on it even though I have not used it much. Then some years later, I finally throw it away.

This can get very expensive very quickly. It can also be a bit depressing. We think the new possession will make us happy and we are quickly disappointed. Very rarely do we find ourselves looking back fondly on a purchase we made a year ago. With experiences, we can re live them and retell them as stories, and often we have learned something from the experience. This may be learning about a new sport or activity, a new country, or different and interesting ways to approach something. We may also learn something about ourselves. A classic example we see in reality TV shows where the contestant overcomes a fear by ski diving or bungee jumping. Of course, in our own lives, the lesson can be more diverse and personal to us.

Of course, we can also get accustomed to an experience. If we ski dive every day, or live on a tropical island, we quickly adjust to our new reality. We are really talking about once off or less regular experiences that we do not adjust to, as compared to a lifestyle change. This we will talk about in other sections. Our misconception around comparing experiences with materialistic purchases is that we think an experience will be over in an hour, day, or week, where a materialistic purchase will last forever. This section is attempting to show this comparison from a different perspective in the hope you will appreciate the value of an experience next time you are making a decision. When we do decide to choose between an experience and a material possession, we need to keep in mind, not just the monetary value, but things like the social advantages, personal satisfaction and growth, new perspectives, etc.

> *"It is only in adventure that some people succeed in knowing themselves - in finding themselves"*
> *Andre Gide*

Dr. Thomas Gilovich a psychology professor at Cornell University, has been looking for a link between money and happiness. He says, "We buy things to make us happy, and we succeed. But only for a while. New things are exciting to us at first, but then we adapt to them." This is the classic Hedonic adaptation as mentioned earlier. Gilovich says, "I'm not saying you should never reward a couple of hard weeks at work with a new outfit and a night out, but our larger investments should go toward experiences that create lifelong memories rather than an item that will lose its "cool" factor within a few years (if it's lucky)." He also has said, "Our experiences are a bigger part of ourselves than our material goods. You can really like your material stuff. You can even think that part of your identity is connected to those things, but nonetheless, they remain separate from you. In contrast, your experiences really are part of you. We are the sum total of our experiences."

So when you think of an experience, do not think of the cost, think of the fun, adventure, excitement, and of course, the memory! Also keep in mind that the outcome or the actual experience itself is harder to predict than a material object. When enjoying an experience, we may make new friends, have a life changing breakthrough of thought, or find a new sport hobby or interest. It is the other intangible and unpredictable side of experiences that make them so exciting.

# Chapter 33

## The subconscious mind

*"The conscious mind may be compared to a fountain playing
in the sun and falling back into the great subterranean
pool of subconscious from which it rises"*
*Sigmund Freud*

Like a supercomputer, our subconscious mind is extremely powerful in delivering results that we require. The catch, however, is that unlike a supercomputer where we can type in information to extract an answer, our subconscious mind works at a more emotional level. Our subconscious mind needs to hear from our conscious mind in ways that are less tangible than what we understand in everyday life. This is where the power of meditation and other techniques come from. This is where the power of a clear vision can be harnessed to help us in our everyday life.

Our perception of the world is a reflection of our mental filter and our subconscious interpretation of what we see, hear, touch, and smell. It only stands to reason that we can alter our perception of the world. When we alter our perception of the world, we can actually change our physical relationship to that world. When we perceive our world to be working for us, to be giving us what we need to accomplish what we want, it lives up to that reality. It is a self-fulfilling prophecy that is based on logic and science.

## The Red Car

When I was young, I was in search of a new car, well not new, but new for me at least. I found a red Cortina, a mid-sized sedan. I thought red could be a good color for a car, because I don't seem to remember seeing many of them around, so would be easy to find in the supermarket car park. Plus, red looked good, it seemed a bit different. That day on the way home, I saw red cars everywhere. Has this ever happened to you? You may have been saying to a friend that you never see police cars on the road any more, or that you haven't noticed any hitchhikers recently. On the way home, you see three police cars and a hitchhiker on the side of the road. This can happen to us in all sorts of ways. It may happen regarding job opportunities, community events, or anything else that we don't notice on a day-to-day basis. It feels like some kind of magic or coincidence. Some people even get a little bit freaked out when this happens.

The reason this happens is simple. Every day we are exposed to thousands of sights, sounds, and smells. We are also bombarded by thoughts feelings and emotions. Our minds have little chance to notice, and less chance to remember, all these things. It has been suggested that our brain receives eleven million pieces of information every second, and that it can only process 40 bits per second. The exact data has been up for discussion by researchers and philosophers. The message, however, is simple. There is so much more information out there that we are exposed to than we can possibly process. This means we have to decide which bits to take notice of.

This is not something that happens on a conscious level. It is a subconscious filter. Not only does our subconscious manage this filter, it allows us to complete tasks automatically. Things that we do every day become automatic and habitual. We don't even have to think about breathing, walking, when we are thirsty, etc. Even more impressive is our ability to do more complex tasks automatically. We may be able to drive the kids to school or drive to work, hang out the washing, even do the shopping almost completely automatically. This is a major accomplishment for the human mind. It allows our brains to be freed up, so we can process other, more pressing information. When we are driving the kids to school, we may be planning what's for dinner that night, whom we need to call, bills we need to pay.

For those of you who are car enthusiast, or who know me well, my first car was a Holden Brougham, the red Cortina was my third car. The Brougham, was gold in colour and I even had a gold tow ball! I spoke about perspective before. Well perspective weaves into this idea of the mental filter. This gold Holden Brougham, to me was a mix between a Rolls

141

Royce and a Porsche. When I drove it I was on top of the world. From my perspective I was driving the best car on the road (I since have found this is common among first car drivers).

This helped with my mental filter, because I did not feel inferior to someone driving a Porsche or Rolls Royce. I was one of them, a part of the club. Sure this was driven by ignorance, but according to my subconscious I was up there with the best. It gave me a lot of self-confidence. It allowed me to move on from any issues I had with self-confidence at school. Without the fear, or any issues with self-esteem, I was able to notice people and things in my environment that were in line with my dreams and desires. I was free to see the world as I wanted it, to really enjoy the time I had.

Our subconscious mind, once we take away all the obstacles, give it clear directions and let it know what we really want, is able to work wonders.

## The Invisible Gorilla

Our brains, it has been proven, work on a very narrow filter. When we are going through our day-to-day life, our minds filter everything else out except for what is important to us. We filter everything out that is not required to achieve our immediate aims and future goals. Our mind is so efficient and effective in this area that we can completely ignore things that may seem blatantly obvious to other people.

This is more scientifically called change blindness. These failures to notice large changes to scenes suggest that we are aware of far less of our visual world than we think. Related studies explore what aspects of our environment automatically capture attention, and what objects and events go unnoticed. Such studies reveal the surprising extent of unintentional blindness, otherwise known as perceptual blindness; "The failure to notice unusual and salient events in their visual world, when attention is otherwise engaged and the events are unexpected."[146] Other research includes, "Scene perception, object recognition, visual memory, visual fading, attention, and driving and distraction."[147]

In one famous study by Simons and Chabris, The Invisible Gorilla,[148] participants were asked to watch two groups of people passing a basketball. Six people, three in white shirts and three in black shirts, passed basketballs around. While they watched, they were told to keep a silent count of the number of passes made by the people in white shirts. At some point, a gorilla strolls into the middle of the action, dressed in black, faces the camera and thumps its chest, and then leaves, spending nine seconds on screen. Would you see the gorilla? Almost everyone has the intuition that the answer is "yes, of course I would." How could something so obvious go completely unnoticed? But when Simons and Chabris did this experiment at Harvard University several years ago, they found that half of the people who watched the video and counted the passes missed the gorilla. It was as though the gorilla was invisible. This experiment reveals two things: that we are missing a lot of what goes on around us and that we have no idea that we are missing so much.

Simons and Chabris did another experiment along the same lines; the door study. A researchers went to the streets to ask people directions. The researcher would stand there talking to an unsuspecting passerby asking for directions. Halfway through the discussion, two people carrying a door passed between them. As the door passed, one of the people carrying the door traded place with the researcher. The person who was halfway through giving directions did not notice that the person he was talking to had completely changed. You can find more information about both these studies and further information on this topic at www.theinvisiblegorilla.com.

What the red car example, and these studies clearly show, is that we do not take notice of many things around us. We notice the things we are thinking about and ignore the rest. It only stands to reason therefore, that everyone sees, fears, and smells the world slightly differently. You can quickly see why it is said that "Everyone sees the world differently." You only need to talk to your friends or people you meet about what they see in the world or what they notice, the signs and advertisements, the information they consume. It becomes very personal to that person. When I worked in IT and Telecommunications and drove into the city in the mornings, I noticed all the Teco billboards and signs. Rarely did I notice anything to do with handbags or shoes!

This is how having a clear vision of what you want to achieve becomes so powerful. If you have a written vision or a vision board that you refer to often, you are priming your mind to open its filter to let in objects and opportunities that will help you achieve your goals. When you are clear on what you need, your mind is open and accepting of these things. Your mind will consciously or subconsciously pick up subtle or not-so-subtle information that is in line with your dream. If you really think about it, you will see how powerful this can become. We know that our subconscious mind is extremely powerful and an effective tool to help us if we can learn to use it. Our subconscious mind needs very clear direction and instructions on what it has to do.

## Noticing the negative

Conversely, if we do not have a clear vision of what we want, if our perception of the world is negative and unsupportive, this is how we will perceive the world. In the case where we are always talking and thinking about the negative, like when the red car appears in our vision, negative circumstances will be all we see. You can see how this view of the world can spiral downward very quickly. If we are not giving clear directions to our subconscious on what we want, need, and are most passionate about, we can easily be giving the wrong information. We can easily be giving information that is not conducive to a successful and happy life.

We all have known a critic, the judge, the procrastinator, or other traits that live inside us. This little voice, the negative one that takes up 80% of our thinking, is extremely powerful. When we focus on what we want, we actively bring things into our lives. We can then take advantage of the situations and resources they provide.

When we recognize our inner critic, we are in a better position to do something about it. By simply acknowledging that there is a negative voice within us, we can make a conscious effort to listen to it. The more we listen to it, the better we understand it. Often, as we all know, the voice goes around and around and around in our head. It becomes so annoying sometimes that we turn to drugs, alcohol, or other devices to quieten the noise. Even worse is if we don't even realize that it's happening.

Try an experiment; for one day, make a mental note of any time you hear the inner voice, when it criticizes, judges, or tries to negatively impact something we are trying to accomplish. You will quickly find that we are very good at dwelling on the negative. As you begin to practice listening to it and build your positive intelligence and attitudes, you will find the inner critic will quieten down considerably. It pays to actively work at reducing the inner critic and give it less power. The best way to do this is to know it exists and to work to reduce it.

This is why we should use all the tools and techniques available to us to build our happiness, positivity, and resources for success. Some practices, without this basic understanding of how our minds work, may seem like a waste of time. It is far too intangible for our conscious mind to understand the deeper workings of our subconscious.

# Chapter 34
## The Less Tangible

*"The mind is everything, we understand - What you think, you become"*
*Buddha*

The red car and the invisible gorilla give us an insight into our minds from a scientific perceptive. The science can clearly explain why we all perceive the world slightly differently. It explains why we don't see some things and even how some events, whilst seeming like coincidence, may only be a physical manifestation of our minds picking up something that is important to us. That said, of course ourselves, our minds and the larger world itself, are a lot more complex than that. Whilst the science can explain many causes and effects to great detail, there is a whole dimension that is operating in conjunction with these processes.

Great minds through the centuries have understood the power of the less tangible and the power we can receive by contemplating and thinking about what we want to achieve. By setting clear intentions to our subconscious, to our higher power (whatever that may mean to you), and the universe, we have a far greater chance of succeeding in all domains of life. These may include social, occupational, physical, or financial factors. By listening to what modern science and the great thinkers and religions from the dawn of time have to say, we are in a much better position to get where we want to go. Of course, there are way too many quotes and passages that support this view than could fit into one book. Some call it the law of attraction, or the law of reciprocity, others look at it from other perspectives.

The support or commitment for this law from the great minds is unquestionable. The results have been proven time and time again. Sometimes these results can be explained and sometimes they cannot.

Sometimes we are able to apply logic and meaning to what has happened around us. Sometimes we just have to take it on faith. This book is not intended to sway anyone's higher level faith or beliefs in any way. What I will try to point out is there is a consistency in the teachings of the religions, philosophers, success writers, and other great minds. If we can accept this consistency, and harness the power we may gain from it, we are better empowered to believe in, and use to our advantage some of the better understood tools and techniques to improve our lives.

Let's look at some of the ancient wisdom that supports the view that what you think about will become reality. The Bible tells us - "For as he thinks within himself, so he is." Proverbs 23:7. It is also written in Matthew 21:22 - "And whatever you ask in prayer, you will receive, if you have faith." There is also a well-known proverb "As ye sow, so shall ye reap."

From the Buddha, "The mind is everything, we understand - What you think, you become," Which is a summarization of the much longer text, Dvedhavitakka Sutta: Two Sorts of Thinking. Also from the Buddhist tradition, "All that we are, is the result of what we have thought: it is founded on our thoughts, it is made up of our thoughts. If a man speaks or acts with an evil thought, pain follows him, as the wheel follows the foot of the ox that draws the carriage. If a man speaks or acts with a pure thought, happiness follows him, like a shadow that never leaves him." One more from the Buddhist tradition states, "It is good to tame the mind, which is difficult to hold in and flighty, rushing wherever it listeth; a tamed mind brings happiness." Also "[What we] think and ponder upon becomes the inclination of our minds."

The Sikh Gurus Prophet-Masters have this to say, "Clearly, our thoughts have great power over our life. This statement -As you think, so you become - which all the wise ones agree on, is at the core of true understanding as to how our thinking affects who we are. It also highlights the connection between what we think and what we ultimately become."[149]

Some years ago, the late Nobel prize-winning Dr. Albert Schweitzer was asked by a reporter, "Doctor, what's wrong with men today?" The great doctor was silent a moment, and then he said, "Men simply don't think!" Marcus Aurelius, the great Roman Emperor, said, "A man's life is what his thoughts make of it."

Heraclitus, a pre-Socratic Greek philosopher said, "Day by day, what you choose, what you think and what you do is who you become."

Benjamin Disraeli, former British Prime Minister said this, "Everything comes if a man will only wait... a human being with a settled purpose must accomplish it, and nothing can resist a will that will stake even existence for its fulfillment." He also said, "Action may not always bring happiness; but there is no happiness without action."

There are many great success writers. A few of the most famous and their books, that I highly recommend are; Stephen R. Covey -The 7 Habits of Highly Effective People, Jack Canfield -The Success Principles, Dale Carnegie - How to make friends and influence people and T. Harv Eker - Secrets of the Millionaire Mind. These are all well-known books and authors. The common theme amongst all these authors, or I should more correctly say, great thinkers, is that they all believe that to make change, you must first know what you want and think about it all the time.

Arguably, the father of success principles and thinking is Napoleon Hill. He founded the motivational movement and much of the works in this field are an adaptation of his early works. For this reason, I would like to share with you a quote and poem, from Mr. Hill. He was a great believer of needing to think what you want before it will manifest in your life. Hence the name of his arguably most famous book, Think and Grow Rich. If you do not read any other books on success principles, I highly recommend this one. Other great books by Napoleon Hill include; The Law of Success, Napoleon Hill's Golden Rules, The Magic Ladder to Success, the list goes on. His writings are dated at an earlier time, yet his principles, tools, and techniques are still relevant today. "Set your mind on a definite goal and observe how quickly the world stands aside to let you pass." Napoleon Hill, Think and Grow Rich.

*"If you think you are beaten, you are,*
*If you think you dare not, you don't.*
*If you like to win, but you think you can't,*
*It is almost certain you won't.*

*If you think you'll lose, you're lost,*
*For out in the world we find,*
*Success begins with a fellow's will -*
*It's all in the state of MIND.*

— *Napoleon Hill, Think and Grow Rich*

Whether you believe the words of Napoleon Hill, the Bible, the Buddhist traditions, or any number of great thinkers, or can follow the logic of modern science, it should be crystal clear to you that what you think in your mind has the ability to change your physical reality.

Whether you want to become rich, successful at work and life, live a happy and meaningful life, enjoy close relationships, or just want to have fun, you should first set that intention. You can do that by writing, drawing, pasting pictures on a vision board, or with any manner you choose. The more emotion and passion you can muster, the better. The more you can believe that what you want is possible, even if it seems remote, the better. The stronger your commitment and deep desire is to fulfill your dreams, the greater chance of them becoming reality.

The stumbling block for many people in this regard is working out, using their current knowledge and logic, how they will achieve their dreams. The most important part is not to know how it will happen just yet, but to know what it is and why you want it. Your 'why' becomes your passion and your drive, the 'what' becomes your direction.

By setting the intention, the direction, the outline of where you want to go, you are setting yourself up to find the knowledge, to find the answer, to discover the currently invisible resources available to you. We live in a world of abundance. There is so much available to you that you do not see or know of yet. By changing your mindset and perspective, you open yourself to an increasing world of opportunity and possibilities.

# Chapter 35

## *80/20 rule*

*"For many events, roughly 80% of the effects come from 20% of the causes"*
*Pareto Principle*

The 80/20 principle states that there is an inbuilt imbalance between causes and results, inputs and outputs, and effort and reward. It's more correct name is the Pareto Principle. It states that, for many events, roughly 80% of the effects come from 20% of the causes. We are brought up to believe there is a linear relationship between what we do and what we receive. The reality is, however, significantly different to that. It is more important to pick the right things to work on than to work hard on anything or everything. In business, often that 80% of profit comes from 20% of the customers.

Both the chaos theory and the 80/20 principle show that the universe is in fact unbalanced, and non-linear and cause-and-effect are rarely linked in an equal way. They state that forces can self-organize and that the more powerful forces will take more of their share of resources. Both these theories talk about feedback loops and how a small influence can be greatly multiplied using feedback loops to produce highly unexpected results. Often when you start something, it takes time to gain momentum; we see only small changes at the beginning that at some point, the tipping point, a small amount of extra effort can reap huge returns.

Pareto discovered that 80% of Italy's land was owned by 20% of the population. He then began to discover that this was true in many other areas. Research shows us that the top 20% of populations have 80% of the wealth. The concept applies to many areas of life. 80% of our problems are caused by 20% of our actions. 80% of our success will come from 20% of our activity. 80% of accidents come from 20% of hazards, the list goes on.

The real key of the 80/20 rule is to take resources from the 80% that are providing you with only 20% gain and allocating those resources to the 20% that is providing 80% of the gain.

Richard Koch has written an excellent book explaining this principle-The 80/20 Principle: The Secret to Achieving More with Less. It explains in detail how you can utilize this principle to achieve more in everyday life. He writes -

The 80/20 principle says we should;

- Celebrate exceptional productivity rather than praise a rich effort
- Look for a short cut, rather than run the full course
- Exercise control over our lives with the least possible effort
- Be selective, not exhaustive
- Strive for excellence in a few things, rather than a good performance in many
- Delegate or outsource as much as possible, especially if you can get a tax deduction
- Choose our carers and employers with extraordinary care
- Only do the things we are best at doing and enjoy the most
- Look beneath the normal texture of life to uncover ironies and oddities
- Always look for the 20% of effort that will give you 80% of returns
- Calm down, work less, and target a limited number of valuable goals with a principal; will it work for you, rather than pursuing every available opportunity
- Make the most of your lucky strengths when we are at our peak and the stars are aligned.

Much of the 80/20 rule is in line with the concepts within this book. By carefully planning our lives, by understanding what our goals are and what our ultimate dream is, we are setting ourselves up to take advantage of the Pareto principle. We are identifying positive plans that do not include winding around the obstacles. We are identifying our true passions and what's really important in our life. This way, we are less likely to waste our time on unimportant tasks. We are less likely to spend time and energy on tasks that are not in line with our true purpose. We are not living a life to be busy for the sake of been busy. Our actions have purpose and meaning. This is the 80/20 rule.

As long as we are aware of this principle, and take note to see where it is applied in our lives, we can take advantage of it. If we actively look for areas where our efforts are not giving us maximum gain, we can change or not even complete these tasks. When we notice the areas where 20% of our effort gives 80% of our results, we can focus to develop these areas. The 80/20 principle is extremely powerful and we should look for ways to live our life, to create our plans, and our goals to fully utilize it.

# Chapter 36

## Happiness Inside and Out

*"The main goal of life is happiness"*
*Dalai Lama*

### Lessons from the Dalai Lama

I have heard the Dalai Lama talk live in a large stadium in Melbourne, Australia, many years ago. I remember he kept repeating two words "Happy life." His message was simple and inspirational. He did not focus too much on any religion or belief. He simply reinforced and explained his idea that has been repeated by him many times, "The main goal of life is happiness."

To understand what he means by "happiness," we should explore the Buddhist understanding of Sukha. It is Sanskritis term that can be defined as; "A state of flourishing that arises from mental balance and insight into the nature of reality. Rather than a fleeting emotion or mood aroused by sensory and conceptual stimuli, sukha is an enduring trait that arises from a state of mental balance. It entails a conceptually unstructured and unfiltered awareness of the true nature of reality."[150]

As the Tibetan teacher Yongey Mingyur Rinpoche writes in The Joy of Living, "Unfortunately, one of the main obstacles we face when we try to examine the mind is a deep-seated and often unconscious conviction that we're born the way we are and [there is] nothing we can do can change that."[151]

According to Buddhism, the state we generally consider to be 'normal' is just a starting point and not the goal that we ought to be setting for ourselves. The Buddhist tradition has a heavy focus on the development of the mind. In fact, much time is spent reading and chanting ancient text. These are exercises to build the muscles of the mind. The Buddhist

*Michael Hunt*

tradition tells us that this training of the mind is extremely important. Like the muscles of our body, our mind should be trained to increase its ability. This concept has been more recently proven in the field of neuroscience. We now know that the way we use our brain can make physical changes within it. As stated in Happiness: A Guide to Developing Life's Most Important Skill, "Each of us has the potential to become free from mental states that cause suffering for ourselves and others, to find inner peace and to contribute to the well-being of others. But just wishing for this is not enough. We need to train our minds."[152]

Cross-cultural studies[153] have clearly demonstrated that, "In accordance with Buddhist views, the pursuit of extrinsic, materialistic values is detrimental to well-being. These studies define 'consumerism' as a mindset that makes one believe that a happy, meaningful, and successful life occurs when a person is wealthy and owns many possessions that convey a high social status."

Happiness, from the Buddhist perspective, is not gained through physical possessions. It is gained by developing peace and happiness through mental training. We live in a modern world and sometimes feel that these traditions are from a previous time. That worldly goods and consumption of products in this new world can in fact lead us to happiness. This viewpoint has been proven by many studies to be incorrect. This includes studies published in The High Price of Materialism, that state: "People in a variety of settings have shown that to the extent people take on consumerist beliefs, the more they report high levels of personal suffering, of depression and anxiety, as well as physical discomfort (headaches, stomach aches, and backaches). They also report stronger, more frequent experiences of unpleasant emotions such as anger, frustration, sadness, anxiety, and worry. Materialistic values are also associated with using more drugs such as alcohol, tobacco, and other mind-altering substances."[154]

There are a wide range of studies that back these claims. It should not be surprising; we all know that the joy of purchases can quickly fade. We know how little satisfaction we really get from materialistic behavior. How much more satisfying is it when we get out and enjoy life with other people? One study showed that "Materialistic individuals report engaging in fewer pro-social and more anti-social activities, including questionable ethical behaviors in business settings."[155] There are benefits of more social environments and behavior focusing on others and experiences. Abundant research shows that intrinsic goals are positively associated with personal, social, and ecological well-being. Studies have shown, "People oriented towards intrinsic values are more empathic, more cooperative, and more likely to engage in the kinds of pro-social, generous behaviors that promote good will and the well-being of others."[156]

Buddhism argues that there is no direct relationship between pleasure and happiness. This in large part is due to "hedonic adaptation" which is to say that, when we keep experiencing something that gives us pleasure, it quickly looses the effect. Such as when we eat the vanilla ice cream, the first few mouthfuls taste great, then after a while, we hardly taste it. In fact, it becomes just calories. We adjust quickly to any such pleasure. In contrast, true happiness is long lasting.

The collaborative research between neuroscientists and Buddhists seems to support this distinction between pleasure and happiness. The mental states that are achieved by people who commit to meditation practices find emotional balance and positive affects (involving, for instance, the left prefrontal cortex), rather than with sensations and pleasure (involving the reward areas of the brain). For the Dalai Lama, happiness does not consist of an uninterrupted succession of pleasurable experiences. Rather, it is an optimal way of being, an exceptionally healthy state of mind that underlies all emotional states, that embraces the joys and sorrows that come our way. It is also a state of wisdom and of insight, as we better understand our true nature of reality. "Sukha includes a combination of various fundamental human qualities, such as altruistic love, compassion, inner peace, inner strength, and inner freedom."[157]

According to Buddhism, there is a direct relationship between having a good heart and happiness. Joy and satisfaction are closely tied to love and affection. As for misery, it goes hand in hand with selfishness and hostility. The research in neuroscience also indicates that loving kindness and compassion are among the most positive of all positive emotions or mental states. According to Buddhism, "Cultivating loving kindness and compassion is essential to happiness."[158]

The Dalai Lama also stresses the fact that, "Compassion is a source of courage in the face of suffering. When we experience in a self-centered way, either our own suffering or others' sufferings, the greater those sufferings are, the more discouraged we will become. Conversely, if we are deeply concerned with others' well-being and not overly focused upon ourselves, our own sufferings will seem flimsy; and the more we are exposed to others' sufferings, the more our compassionate courage to do whatever it takes to dispel these sufferings will grow."[159]

# Emotions

The real strength in Buddhism is the ability to control emotion. This is achieved through all the mental training. The more we can accept the reality of our situation and actively change our thoughts and emotions to better deal with that situation, the better the outcome. According to the Dalai Lama, "One important aspect of the 'Buddhist science' of happiness is to develop methods for dealing skilfully with emotions, reinforcing constructive ones and counteracting afflictive ones. Buddhism considers that if an emotion strengthens our inner peace and seeks the good of others, it is positive, or constructive; if it shatters our serenity, deeply disturbs our mind and is intended to harm others, it is negative, or afflictive."[160] This is why it's so important to build our positive emotions. As we are building our positive emotions in our own personal way, we are training our minds. We do not all need to retreat into the mountains for years of meditative and mind-developing practices. We should however, put in place our own practices that fit within our own lifestyles. By actively understanding our emotions, and working to create more positivity and happiness in our lives, we are in a much better position to transform our lives and create new possibilities for success.

The Dalai Lama said, "Recognition of the nature of the mind and an accurate understanding of the phenomenal world are essential for our quest for happiness. If the mind relies on totally erroneous views about the nature of things and maintains them, it will be very difficult for us to transform ourselves and achieve freedom. Developing a correct view is not a question of faith or adherence to dogma but of clear understanding. This arises from a correct analysis of reality. The clearer our view of reality and the more positive we are toward the future, the less ability our minds have to dwell on negative, unsupported assumptions, beliefs, thoughts, and emotions."

# Chapter 37

## Our Environment

*"We adapt to the environment we put ourselves in"*
*Michael Hunt*

### The Benefits of Contact with Nature

*"The enjoyment of scenery employs the mind without fatigue*
*and yet exercises it; tranquilizes it and yet enlivens it; and thus,*
*through the influence of the mind over the body, gives the effect*
*of refreshing rest and reinvigoration to the whole system"*
*Frederick Law Olmsted (the father of American landscape architecture)*

Experiencing contact with nature is a great way to find peace and serenity. Nature allows us to clear our minds of the hassles of everyday life. It is nonthreatening and the way we relate to it is different to a city full of buildings and billboards. Many of us spend hours in our own gardens creating a space of beauty and peace. We love our gardens, because we feel safe and at home. As we watch our gardens grow, it is easier to be in touch with the natural world. Personally, I enjoy maintaining a vegetable garden. Nowadays, I prefer to keep it small and manageable. Getting outside and watching the vegetables grow gives me much pleasure. When connecting with the garden, I find it easier to let my mind rest and forget my troubles.

I am not alone on this; studies have found that people exposed to nature, or even views of nature, tend to be happier and healthier. Perhaps the best-known study of this sort, published in Science, 1984, found that "Gallbladder surgery patients randomly assigned to rooms with a window view of a natural setting (i.e., some trees) had significantly shorter hospital stays (7.96 versus 8.7 days post-op), fewer negative comments about their condition recorded by nurses, fewer minor complications, and had a lower need for painkillers than patients whose windows faced a brown brick wall."

A study of Michigan prisoners randomly assigned to cells facing either the prison courtyard or rolling farmland found, "A 24% higher rate of sick calls among those whose cells faced inward, toward the prison yard."[161] Other studies directly assess anxiety and stress responses, as well as behavioral impacts of nature. Dental patients, for instance, "Reported less anxiety and had lower blood pressure when a mural of a nature scene was hung in the waiting room than on days when it was removed."[162]

There is more to this than just a nice feeling. These studies show that access to nature, or even just a view of nature, provides a significant measurable positive effect. Some studies even show that cognitive function can improve simply by enjoying nature. One such study showed that "Performance on tasks like proofreading seems to improve from viewing nature scenes, as does attention, alertness, and focus."[163]

Time in nature can be great when incorporated into mindfulness and meditation practices. The peaceful and serene environments lend themselves to a peaceful mind. Even getting away from your desk or outside the house for a brief 10 minute walk can refresh the mind and invigorate the senses, so you're ready to take on the next challenge of the day

<u>Lost</u>
*Stand still.*
*The trees ahead and the bushes beside you Are not lost.*
*Wherever you are is called Here,*
*And you must treat it as a powerful stranger,*
*Must ask permission to know it and be known.*
*The forest breathes. Listen. It answers,*
*I have made this place around you,*
*If you leave it you may come back again, saying Here.*

*David Whyte, The Heart Aroused: Poetry and the*
*Preservation of the Soul in Corporate America*

# The Stanford Prison Experiment -
# We Adapt to our Environment

The Stanford prison experiment is a well-known experiment that is referenced in many research papers to show how quickly we adapt to the environment in which we live. After reading about this experiment funded by the military and run by a researcher, Zimbardo, I could better understand how people living in different situations quickly adapt to their environment. This is equally true for people living among the golf club scene as it is for the street beggar. Often due to situations beyond their control, people's lives change drastically. It is eye opening to read this experiment and understand how quickly we accept our new reality.

The experiment was conducted in 1971 by a team of researchers using college students. The students were put into a simulated prison environment, some assigned as guards and some assigned as prisoners. It was only a matter of days until the students assigned to being guards started behaving like guards in a very real way. The same also went for the students allocated as prisoners

The study found that the participants adapted to their roles well beyond the researchers' expectations, "As the guards enforced authoritarian measures and ultimately subjected some of the prisoners to psychological torture. Many of the prisoners passively accepted psychological abuse and, at the request of the guards, readily harassed other prisoners who attempted to prevent it. The experiment even affected Zimbardo himself, who, in his role as the superintendent, permitted the abuse to continue."[164] What this experiment showed clearly is that we adapt to our environment extremely quickly and effectively. It is almost scary to read about the experiment in detail and how easily we are changed by our environment.

If you are feeling that the life that you are living does not sit well with you or is not what you really wanted from life, it is worth questioning the reality in which you are living. Was this reality chosen by you? Or did you just fall into it? This is why it is so powerful to verify your own vision of life. To take the time to think deeply about the sort of life you want to enjoy. To understand the discrepancy between your current reality and the life you would like to live. We are very sensitive to our environment in ways that may not seem obvious. We can use this knowledge to better enhance our lifestyle in a positive way. This may require a major lifestyle change or small adjustments. By making some simple changes around our home and building in time each day to experience nature, even if it is just a walk around the block, we can greatly increase our chance of finding peace and happiness.

# Chapter 38

# Self -limiting beliefs and behaviors

*"What we can or cannot do, what we consider possible or
impossible, is rarely a function of our true capability. It is
more likely a function of our beliefs about who we are"*
*Tony Robbins*

Our biggest obstacles to success are our self-limiting beliefs. We all
have them. There are thousands of books on success specifically designed
to break down our self-limiting beliefs. These self-limiting beliefs, in part,
are automatically broken down by using the foundation to success. By
verifying your vision, setting specific goals, creating plans, and taking
action, you are mentally preparing yourself to overcome these self-limiting
beliefs. The reason self-limiting beliefs cause us such problems is because
of the power we give to our negative thoughts. We know when we start to
think about something we wish to achieve, we automatically look for the
reasons why we should not go for our goal.

I have discussed general principles and ideas on how to overcome
limiting beliefs. By accepting the power negative thoughts have over us, and
using the tools available, we are able to overcome many obstacles. So what
can we do when one of our self-limiting beliefs creates an insurmountable
obstacle? Many times, when this is the case, it is a deep-rooted obstacle that
we have lived with for a long time. Many of these obstacles are addictive
by nature. Some of them are due to mental illness.

When we are experiencing such serious obstacles in our life, we should
think seriously about searching for outside assistance. This is not always
the preferred option. It makes us feel uncomfortable and uneasy.

If you are in this situation, deep down you know something must be
done with this self-limiting belief or behavior. If you really want to live a

fulfilling and happy life, you must face your demons! Can you be successful while harboring self-limiting beliefs, addictions, or mental illness? You can be to a point. I know many people in the corporate world who are very successful in their jobs, while maintaining addictions, self-limiting beliefs, or dealing with mental illness. In fact, many successful people in business, music, sports, and the arts have highly strung, addictive, or bipolar personalities. You do not need to look far to find these people.

The trouble, however, is that often people with these personalities, whilst successful in one domain, completely fail in others. Even those who appear to be successful in many domains ultimately will pay the price. On a personal note, I have struggled with alcoholism my whole life. I was successful at work, successful raising my family, and had an active social life. Somewhere in my mid-forties, the cracks began to appear. The drinking was less enjoyable than it once was. The benefits no longer outweighed the costs. I was drinking way too much, and for many years, knew something had to be done. As with any alcoholic, I did not take action until the reality of my situation was staring me in the face. I endured much internal debate, of course, most of that focusing on the negatives of giving up drinking. I was a real-life example of the fact that 80% of our thoughts are negative. I spent so much time worrying about how hard it would be to give up, how much of a struggle social situations would become, and thought I would never be able to relax again after a long day's work. How could I come home from a long stressful day and not have a drink to relax me?

How wrong I was. I reached out for external help and found a 12 step program that was cheap and easy to attend. I stopped drinking that very day! To my complete and utter amazement, over the next few months, I became more relaxed than I ever had been. I found peace of mind and serenity. With all the focus on the negative, I had never thought about all the positive sides to not drinking. Giving up was a lot easier than I thought, social situations became easier without always looking for a drink, and I was so relaxed after work because my mind was at peace. Maintaining sobriety over the years has had its challenges. I have had a couple of relapses. Fortunately, each one was short, and knowing how easy it was initially to give up, I had no trouble finding sobriety again. Contrary to my initial belief that being sober I would become boring and unexcited, my life has been on an upward spiral ever since. I cannot tell you how many people I have meet with similar stories to mine, they are everywhere.

I am not here to preach to anyone. Everyone has their own demons and needs to deal with them in their own personal way. What I do hope to convey is that it is not until you try to deal with your demons, your self-limiting beliefs that you will ever know how much power they really have on you. We spend so much time and energy avoiding the topic. We rarely ask the question, can I overcome it? Please take some time to imagine your life without your self- limiting beliefs. Imagine your life without your addictions, your depression, or other obstacles getting in your way. Take some time to visualize your life without these self-limiting beliefs and obstacles.

Governments, non-profit organizations, clubs, and groups are everywhere to help you deal with all kinds of obstacles. They are not there to hassle you and tell you where you have gone wrong. They are there because they work. Whatever problem you have, there has been someone before you who has overcome it. There is someone available to help you as long as you are willing to put out your hand.

I once heard an expert say that there are only three ways to treat depression and other related illnesses; meditation, cognitive therapy, and Prozac. This may sound like a simplistic approach, yet each of these techniques have been proven to be extremely effective. Meditation has been shown, time and time again, to be effective when dealing with depression, addictions, and other self-limiting behaviors.

Cognitive therapy is less understood, yet arguably even more effective. It is defined as "Thoughts, feelings and behavior are all connected, and that individuals can move toward overcoming difficulties and meeting their goals by identifying and changing unhelpful or inaccurate thinking, problematic behavior, and distressing emotional responses. This involves the individual working collaboratively with the therapist to develop skills for testing and modifying beliefs, identifying distorted thinking, relating to others in different ways, and changing behaviors."[165] With cognitive therapy, although many people think of it as something you do with the therapist, it also includes such group sessions as 12 step programs. There are programs widely available and extremely effective, especially group sessions which are generally quick and easy to join. In addition, therapy, something many people would see as a last resort, should be seriously considered if you are unable to overcome an obstacle yourself.

The third option is Prozac. By mentioning Prozac, what is really being referred to here is the use of pharmaceutical solutions. I have direct experience with people who are close to me and clients, who need to manage their depression. I know from this first-hand experience, when it comes to depression and bipolar disorder, pharmaceutical solutions can be very beneficial. In fact, once a person finds the right solution and maintains their dosage correctly, they can live a completely normal life.

Whether you choose the path of meditation, cognitive therapy, a pharmaceutical solution, or any combination, if you stick with it, you will overcome your obstacle. Knowing that there are solutions to overcoming self-limiting beliefs, addictions, and mental disorders, how can anyone afford to live with such conditions? Modern technology, progress, and the increasing ability of the world's smartest people to share information has now put us in a position where help is more effective and more available than ever before. For those dealing with obstacles for a long period of time, they may not know all the advancements that have happened since the last time they reached out for help.

I encourage anyone reading this who is dealing with an obstacle that they are unable to overcome themselves to at least investigate and understand their options. Take the first step and see what happens. When it really comes down to it, except for maybe a bruised ego if you fail, what have you got to lose? Conversely, if you are successful, just imagine the expanding possibilities that have been opened up to you.

# Chapter 39

## The Big Four

*"Freedom is not given to us by anyone; we have to cultivate it ourselves. It is a daily practice... No one can prevent you from being aware of each step you take or each breath in and breathe out"*
*Thich Nhat Hanh*

In this section, we review the big four. Before we do that, let me say, there are many tools and techniques, strategies, and concepts that we can incorporate into our structure of happiness and success. If you are currently using a technique that suits you and your lifestyle, I urge you to keep using it. I encourage you to build it in to your own structure. By ensuring that you are building what works for you, into a solid structure, into your goals, and your plans, you are maximizing the benefit from that technique. If you can re craft a technique that works for you in a way that maximizes positive relationships and/or utilizes your signature strengths, this too is a great way to maximize the benefit from the technique.

This section covers the big four. These techniques are the ones that most often appear in research papers and success books. They are the four techniques that have been shown time and time again to be easy to use and give maximum benefit. If you use no other techniques in your life to increase your happiness and your success, you should aim to at least use two or three of the ones in this section.

In the next section, we will review a wider scope of concepts and techniques that can also be integrated into your structure of success and happiness.

# 1. Train yourself to notice the positive

One of the most useful tools in building your happiness and success is to recognize the positives in your environment. Due to your brain's effective filters, you only take in a very small proportion of the world around you. As you clarify your vision and your goals and focus towards what you want to achieve, it is extremely useful to notice all the positives, especially the ones that are in line with your goals.

## The three good things exercise

An exercise that is fun to do and only takes a few minutes each day is the "Three good things exercise." It helps you build your ability to recognize the positive in everyday life. Each evening, take time to list three positive or good things that happened that day. In my family, we do this at the dinner table with the kids. The kids love it so much, sometimes they will even fight to see who goes first (So much for positivity!). They will often come up with four or five things; they really have fun with it. Some days, I find it easy to find three good things, other days I struggle.

Research tells us if we continue identifying three good things each day for 21 days, we will enjoy lasting benefit. In fact, studies have shown this benefit can last up to 6 months or more. This is a proven, quick, and effective method to train your brain to identify the positives.

The more we can train ourselves to see the positive, the more we can combat that 80% of our internal self-talk that is negative. We are better able to find the positives in what we do. We become better at evaluating challenges and situations from a more neutral perspective.

Building our positivity should not be confused with positive thinking. Building our positivity means seeing things that are real and positive in our environment and in our lives. These things, without training our minds to see them, often go unnoticed. This is the real power of the three good things exercise. As we train our minds to see the positive, we become happier because we better understand and notice the good things around us. Always strive to notice the positive things.

## 2. Build your gratitude

*"Feeling gratitude and not expressing it is like*
*wrapping a present and not giving it."*
William Arthur Ward

Gratitude has consistently been shown to be one of the best tools to enhance one's happiness. It is a great tool to change our perspective of our current environment. Gratitude forces us to be less self-centered and more focused on the bigger picture of life. As we begin to express gratitude, we are also building our gratitude up for what we have in life. When we express gratitude to another person, we generally make them feel better. The idea that making someone else feel better also makes us feel better is well proven. So when we express gratitude, we are also helping ourselves. In addition, as we are more grateful to other people, we are more grateful for what we have. This gratitude helps us to stay in touch with our own reality. That allows us to better see things for how they are. We feel better, and happier, because the positive and good things in life are not simply passing us by.

Research[166] shows "Positive associations between gratitude and measures of positive emotionality, vitality, happiness, satisfaction with life, hope, and optimism." Research has also shown that "A disposition to experience gratitude was negatively related to symptoms of depression and anxiety."[167]

One study examined the associations of subjective well-being and the disposition to experience gratitude. "People with higher satisfaction with life, positive affect, and optimism, and lower depressive symptoms, tended to experience higher levels of gratitude in their daily mood on a day-to-day basis."[168] In another study, Is Gratitude An Alternative To Materialism, researchers showed strong support for the proposition that "Grateful people tend to report being happier, more optimistic, more satisfied with their lives, and less anxious and depressed than do their less grateful counterparts."[169]

In another study of gratitude on happiness, researchers had participants engage in one of three experimental conditions; (a) thinking about someone to whom they felt grateful; (b) writing about someone to whom they felt grateful; or (c) writing a letter to someone to whom they felt grateful. "All three of these experimental conditions led to greater short-term increases in positive affect and greater short-term reductions in negative affect than did a control condition."[170]

## The Gratitude Visit

The Gratitude Visit is when you visit someone who has made a positive impact in your life. You tell them how they have helped you and what impact that has had in your life. This visit helps them and it helps you.

## Daily gratitude

Each day, keep track of what you are grateful for. Some people like to keep a gratitude diary. You can also incorporate this into the three good things exercise. List what went well each day and why you are grateful for it.

## 3. Exercise at least 15 minutes every day.

The effects of exercise are obvious and have been elaborated on in this book. Maintaining at least some form of regular exercise is a mandatory tool for success. The key is to find something that you enjoy doing. If you're exercising to increase your cardiovascular fitness, there are certain requirements that are important to adhere to achieve the results that you want. When it comes to exercising for success, research indicates that the most important factor is regularity. To do anything regularly, ideally you should enjoy it. If the exercise you do for success is the same as you do for cardiovascular fitness or strength, you win the prize. At this point, you are fulfilling the adage "healthy body, healthy mind." Of course, it takes a healthy mind to maintain an exercise regime. It is all interrelated. Find something that you can do regularly that doesn't take a massive amount of self will and go enjoy the benefits. If you find it hard to get out of bed and go for a run, leave your runners next to your bed. If you want to walk at lunchtime, have your runners next to your desk. When you are debating whether you should go for a run, or do some other exercise or not, first put on your shoes or other sports clothes, then decide. The shorter and easier the transition is, the more likely you will be to succeed in that transition. Get creative and have fun with it. If you need motivation, enlist a personal trainer, join the gym or team up with a friend. Your mental and physical health and your success are too important to simply ignore exercise.

## 4. Find a meditation or mindfulness practice that works for you.

I have previously dedicated an entire section to meditation and mindfulness. For this reason, I do not need to further elaborate here. What I will do however is too strongly encourage you to find a meditation or mindfulness practice that suits you and your lifestyle.

If you struggle to identify a practice, may I suggest beginning with the 10 breaths exercise?

Each day, for one month, consciously stop what you are doing and do the 10 breaths exercise. Think of each breath as it comes in and then out. Take special care to notice the pause at the end of the exhale. Try not to think of anything else during this time. If there are thoughts that do enter your mind, do not worry about them. Let them come and let them go. Aim less to stop these thoughts and try more so to not pay them any attention. It is only 10 breaths; you can worry yourself about these things later.

Ideally after an initial practice period, you should aim to do this simple exercise many times each day. Take notice of how you feel before and after the exercise. Do you feel more relaxed? Did you gain any insight? If you do not like the idea of meditation or mindfulness, may I suggest something else? Go for a walk, run, ride or any other activity that could be done on your own. It can be five minutes or fifty minutes, it is up to you. As you set off on your journey, make a deal with yourself. You will either; A; Decide before you go that there is nothing you need to resolve in your mind for the next five minutes (or as long as you go for). Then as you run, walk, or ride, aim not to think about anything, and what thoughts come, let them go just as quickly and easily as they came. Or B; Decide on the one challenge you need a solution for, or the one idea for which you are searching. As you exercise, do not consciously look for the answer. Simply let the thoughts come and go without clinging to any of them, not to think about anything, and to have faith that your subconscious mind will find the answer. Both these options, as simple as they sound, do take some practice. I assure you, if you stick with it and practice regularly, ideally at least 15 minutes a day, you not only will feel better physically, but your mind will begin to co-operate. You will find more peace and naturally discover solutions to everyday problems. You will come up with ideas that your conscious mind could never have come up with no matter how hard you try.

Whether you use the 10 breaths exercise or the physical exercise experiment, you will enjoy the results. As you become better at it, it is worth looking at ways to ensure this becomes regular. You may even find that you wish to extend your practices even further.

# Chapter 40

## Positive Work Programs

*"We not only need to work happy, we need to work at being happy"*
*Shawn Achor*

In this section, we look at an overview of some useful techniques to use in work and life to help drive change. They are listed here and described in more detail below.

1. Utilize internal champions
2. Enter situations that require a positive outcome, when people are well rested and well fed.
3. Capitalize on success
4. Learn from work experiences
5. Learn from personal experience

## 1. Utilize internal champions

When promoting a new program at work, or within a social environment, utilize internal champions. When trying to pitch a new idea, we often spend valuable energy trying to convince the most negative people. We have the idea that, if only I can convince the people who are not supporting me, everyone else will follow. This idea is flawed and risky. How much better would it be to convince and inspire the people who are more inclined to support you? As you build a team of supporters, you are building momentum for your new idea. You're internal champions will naturally propagate the positive aspects of what you are trying to achieve. Ideally, you can use these internal supporters to champion your idea, either informally or formally. Think of how powerful your pitch to the wider business or social community would be if one of the workers, peers or even friends stood up and explained the benefits they would receive in their environment from the new idea or process. As you build support, using the most positive people first, it becomes easier to convince people who are on the fence of the merits of your ideas. Once you begin to convert those people, it becomes easier and easier to sway the people who are less convinced of the idea.

## 2. Enter situations that require a positive outcome when people are well rested and well fed.

Our mind, like any muscle, performs better and is more likely to see the positive when rested and well fed. In one interesting study,[171] researchers found that a judge's willingness to grant parole can be influenced by the time between their latest break and their current hearing. The team studied more than 1,000 parole decisions made by eight experienced judges in Israel over 50 days in a ten–month period. After a snack or lunch break, 65%of cases were granted parole. The rate of favorable rulings then fell gradually, sometimes as low as zero, within each decision session and would return to 65% after a break.

The judges were clearly more upbeat and positive after a break and some food. This has important ramifications for the work (and the home) environment. With this study in mind, do you think you would be most likely to make a sales pitch just before lunch or just after lunch? Should you try to secure a job interview first thing in the morning or straight after lunch, or would it be best just before lunch or at the end of the day? When doing a brainstorming session at your company's annual retreat, should it be left to the end of the day as it often is? Simply by becoming aware that our brain operates much better when it is well rested and the blood is full of glucose and other energy sources, preferably from healthy food, we can drastically increase our success in our work and other life endeavors.

We also know that the mind does get tired. After much thinking, we get to the stage that our brain simply doesn't function as well is it should. With all this in mind, don't you think it would be a great idea when solving complex problems at work to brainstorm the idea first thing in the morning when you are feeling fresh? The added advantage of a brainstorming session first thing in the morning is that our minds have a chance to process what happened during the day. This gives us a great opportunity to come up with additional ideas, or discuss other theories. It also allows our brains time during the day to settle down so we are not thinking about the new idea at home as we are trying to sleep.

## 3. Capitalize on success. Use success to motivate

After a big win at work, or at play, we are often all too quick to get on with the next challenge. It can be extremely powerful to stop and reflect on the recent success. By reflecting on the success, it gives us a chance to congratulate and encourage the people who worked so hard. We have time to review what went well and what we could do better. We build a positive emotion around the success that enhances the memory of that time. By talking about and building on the emotions, the success is better stored in our subconscious to be used at a later time when we need to draw on that energy. Even losses should be reviewed. Often after a loss or a particularly challenging period, we are all too quick to think how bad it went and move on. Often when we look at the experience in hindsight, we can see many things that we actually did well. These things should be acknowledged and remembered. The things that did not go so well should be discussed and remembered. By understanding what did not go so well, we are in a much better position for it not to happen again.

## 4. Learn from work experiences

A common practice in large projects is to perform a post-implementation review. However, as the review takes time and energy, it is often not performed. I spent many years in the corporate world, running large and small telecommunications and IT projects. I have found that when post-implementation reviews are done, it is normally on very large projects and a mandated process required in order to close off the project. Often the learnings, whilst very important, became buried in the post-implementation documents. Or the time and effort to bring all the stakeholders together and discuss what went well and what did not, was often not available. Usually on smaller projects, there was very little post-implementation review. There were simply too many projects to complete and not enough time.

Personally, I found an informal post-implementation review was more effective. Informal chats over a coffee or during lunchtime office barbecues were very effective. By creating informal environments, where most of the project team came together, usually for food or drinks, we created a space to share our learnings, congratulate those who worked so hard and did so well, and encourage those whose performance may have been better. The informal reviews, in my opinion, were much more beneficial than any official review document.

Of course, depending on the size of the organization and the nature of the project, formal reviews that can be shared easily amongst the wider team can be very effective. That said, from my extensive project experience, the lessons were much better shared in the form of a knowledge document, such as a support document or "how to" guide than a "lessons learned" or project review document. Teams are much more likely to search a document full of knowledge than a document stating what has gone wrong. These knowledge documents become worthwhile in respect to time and energy to build, because they can merge the lessons learned plus the experience gained, providing better return for the time spent.

## 5. Learn from personal experience

Although often not done well, the lessons learned processes in business are not uncommon. It is a lot less common in our personal life. When things go well in our life, we usually think "great" and maybe celebrate. How often do we spend time to review how we actually achieved that success? The same when things go wrong. How often do you take the time to think about where the plan took the wrong turn?

We all know the popular quote from Albert Einstein "Insanity: doing the same thing over and over again and expecting different results." So often, when we are not making progress in our life, we keep repeating the same mistakes. Like the person who drinks too much and tells himself "I will stop tomorrow," but tomorrow never comes, the temptations are the same, and they continue. Or the compulsive dieter, who never seems to make progress. Instead of beating ourselves up, and thinking we failed again every day, how much more powerful would it be to understand the lesson learned? We really should have a support document, or "how to" guide for our own lives. I'm not talking about a book like this one, although it is very useful. I am talking about a personal document created by yourself. A document that outlines the very moment you always succumb to temptation, and more importantly, the times you are able to resist it.

Imagine if you had a document of all the successes in your life and what the major contributing factors involved in that success were. Or if you have a document that also includes what has gone wrong in your life including a list of things to take note of, and not to do in the future. Very few of us, no matter how useful it may be, would ever produce such a document. What we can do is to take a little bit of time to think about what went well during our everyday tasks. Like in my informal project review gatherings at work, if we plan our time and a method to review our performance, our successes and failures, it is much more likely to happen. Imagine at the end of each day, week, or on the way to work, you set aside some time to review your progress, what went well and what went wrong.

It has been shown through research and experience that it is better to frame the lesson in a positive way. So if you are struggling with weight loss, for example, focus on what you were doing when it went well. Think rather, not to succumb to temptation, but of something positive that will help you avoid it. If your weakness is snacking on sugary food at work, rather than telling yourself not to snack the unhealthy food, take some healthy food with you and keep it close by.

If you think about what you should not do, you are surely to do it. If you continually think about not eating that chocolate bar in the fridge, that will be on your mind all the time. Rather, if you replace the chocolate bar with a tasty healthy snack, and think about how nice it will be, and healthy for you it is, you are much more likely to succeed. If you are trying to motivate yourself to go for a run, think about how good the fresh air will be, the scenery, or how you will feel once you're finished. If just telling yourself that you should go for a run does not work, think back to Einstein's quote on insanity!

# Chapter 41

## It is all a matter of perspective

*"When you wake up every day, you have two choices. You can either be positive or negative; an optimist or a pessimist. I choose to be an optimist. It's all a matter of perspective"*
*Harvey Mackay*

Have you ever played pool or billiards? If you have, you may have experienced a situation when you played on a really big or very difficult table, then played on an easier table. You may have played on the easier table for years, yet after playing on a harder table or very large table, all of a sudden, you're billiards game becomes really easy. One might think this is because your skill level has been built up on the larger or harder table, yet after years playing on the normal table, a few days on a harder table is not really lifting your ability. You have simply adjusted to the harder reality, and as you go back, it is relatively easier.

I used to row surf boats. Sometimes during training, our coach would throw out the bag. It was a mini parachute that was towed behind the boat. It made it incredibly difficult to move the boat forward. After some time rowing with the bag out the back of the boat, our coach, or sweep as they are known, would then bring the bag in. The first five minutes or so, the rowing would seem very easy. The boat would be flying through the water with what seems like hardly any effort at all. Of course, after rowing with the bag at the back, our muscles are more fatigued than they were before. We have less energy and our technique certainly had not got better.

What changed? We adjusted to the new reality. When the bag was out the back of the boat, it was very hard to pull the oar through the water. Once the bag was removed, the oar moved relatively easily. Of course, it was exactly the same resistance, as before the session with the bag. It was our minds, adjusted to the new reality that now thought it was easier to row.

Rowing was a great experience to learn perspective. Not only by using "the bag" but from the team perspective. When you are in a rowing crew, there are four rowers and a sweep. We trained early mornings, normally at around 5am, as this was the only time we could get everyone in the one place at the one time. If one person did not show up, we could not train and the other four got up at 4:30am, and drove to training for nothing. It was great motivation at this early hour, when you just want to roll over and go back to bed.

We had positions in the boat and we owned these spots, we learnt to row the way that was required for that specific seat and side. We became proud of our commitment to the team. When I was hurting during training and wanted to ease off a bit, I only had to look at the others to understand they too were hurting and I just had to keep going.

We put our pain into perspective. If we train for any sport, if we do it alone, it is harder to keep motivated. If we do not have a specific goal, it is even harder. When we are part of a team and have a specific, challenging goal; to win an event or match, to make it into the state or national championships etc, this is when we will go through all sorts of pain and put is extra effort to succeed. It is our perspective on the pain, on the commitment, that changes, not the actual pain or effort itself. Our change of perspective, makes the pain more bearable and the commitment

> *"Through the oar we work, we sweat*
> *Because for sure it's pain we've met*
> *And which we know you row right through*
> *'Cause you're the stroke of the great "C" crew!"*
> *Michael Hunt – Written for Paul, a member*
> *of our crew, on his birthday card*

Perspective matters in many pursuits. Once, after using running as my exercise for almost a year, I was still running less than 5 km. I found that after about 3 km, I was extremely tired. I found the 5 km very challenging. Once, during a moment of weakness, I agreed to join my wife and some friends in a half marathon. With this new challenge, I realized that I needed to eventually run 21 km. On my very first training session after agreeing to this silly idea, I ran 7 km easily. My perspective had changed from running 5 km to 21 km. Training became easier, whilst longer. I had a specific goal with a clear time frame. When I had originally agreed to running the half marathon, I panicked and thought how hard it would be. I worried whether I would have the motivation, if I could last the distance, or keep up with the required runs each week. As it turned out, the longer and more intense training schedule took less motivation, and I was a lot more regular in my training.

The same can be true in work situations. Remember Parkinson's Law states: *"Work expands so as to fill the time available for its completion."*

We have a certain perspective around what we can achieve each day at work. You may have experienced a time yourself where you had to fill in for a work colleague, were given an additional project to run, were off sick, or going on holidays and you needed to complete more work in less time. Isn't it amazing that often in these situations, we rise to the task? This is especially true when we are motivated in a positive way to accomplish the results. Take for example, when a good friend at work is stuck, and asks you, in our very appreciative tone, to help them out. You have helped each other before and it was always a very positive experience. You set yourself a task to assist them, and you are happy to do so because you know you will be thanked and that you are helping a friend. Contrast this to a work colleague who was just made redundant, or someone you did not like was sick and you had to complete some of their work. When we are positively motivated to take on the extra work, not only does it normally take less time, but we perceive it to take less effort.

When we have a deadline and our whole work team is behind the effort, when we have a shared interest in achieving the target, we can accomplish a lot. It is our perception of the task that makes all the difference. On the other hand, how often have we been ordered to do a task by our boss that we do not understand why we are doing it? When we cannot see the big picture and we think the work will just go to waste! We procrastinate, we stretch the task out, we talk to friends, or search the internet, anything but to complete the task. We may even find ourselves talking negatively about the whole process to our work colleagues. We can potentially bring our work colleagues down too by spreading a negative vibe through the whole office. Whether the task is actually important, we just don't understand, or in fact if it is a waste of time is irrelevant. It is our perception of how important the task is that matters. With our brains' exceptional ability to filter out so much of our world, we often only see one reality. By actively working to understand alternate realities and perspectives, we can quickly put ourselves in a position of applying a more positive perspective to the task. In the example I just mentioned, it may be as simple as asking the boss, why is this so important? That simple question may lead you to be able to approach the task with a positive attitude. This positive attitude then leads to the task being easier and completed quicker. Instead of spreading negativity around the office, you may take it upon yourself to explain to other co-workers why and how important the work you are doing is.

There are always multiple realities and perspectives for any given situation. Like driving home from the supermarket, or walking to the local store, there are often various routes. If we never look for the alternatives, we will never find them. If we actively search for positive perspectives and realities, or the more enjoyable route to our destination, we can significantly increase our happiness and success.

# Chapter 42

## Rituals and habits

*"Our daily decisions and habits have a huge impact upon both our levels of happiness and success"*
*Shawn Achor*

Research tells us that it can take up to 3 months to adopt a habit or ritual. If you would like to start running, save money, read more often, cut television usage, etc., you need to maintain the new habit, or way of living for three months. When transitioning into this new ritual or habit, it is best to focus on the advantages you will receive from this new habit. A future focused approach to any change is extremely beneficial. If you keep thinking about the old way, what you used to do, you will never change. Focus instead on how you will integrate this new habit into your life and the benefits and advantages you will receive from doing so.

If it takes three months to adopt a new habit, that's four new habits every year. Think of how much you can accomplish in any program of change if you adopted four good habits each year. Of course, at the same time, you are leaving behind old behaviors. Four new good habits over the next five years is 20 new good habits. With this number, even if you fall back to some old behavior in some areas of your life, you will surely reap massive rewards. You can transform yourself and discover limitless possibilities in your life by making use of rituals and habits.

Like I said at the beginning of the book, If you put five dollars away every day for 40 years and invested it with a 8% return, you will end up with over half a million dollars. It is the magic of compounding. The first 20 years, you have saved $90,000, and the second 20 years alone gives you

$450,000, a total of $540,000. It's an exponential curve. It is a habit or ritual of saving that pays the dividend!

*"You must acquire the habits and skills of managing a small*
*amount of money before you can have a large amount. Remember,*
*we are creatures of habit and, therefore, the habit of managing*
*your money is more important than the amount"*
T. Harv Eker

Anything in our life that we make a ritual or a habit, whether good and bad, has massive effects over the long term as we climb the exponential curve. Eating an apple a day may not seem much, but over 10 years, that is a lot of apples. Exercising for 15 minutes daily sounds easy, and it is, but if you exercise 15 minutes every day of your life, think of the health benefits. If you wake up just 30 minutes earlier each day, or watch 30 minutes less television, that's 3 1/2 hours every week that you gain to invest in your own development or any other program of action. This adds up to 185 hours each year, nearly 23 days at eight hours a day. That is four or five work weeks, or about a month of work. Think of what you could do with that time. You can learn a new skill, start a new hobby or interest, become better at something you already do, the list goes on. Of course you do not necessarily need to get up half an hour early, or cut out your television. You could utilize your lunch break, find time when you get home from work, or wherever else you can find 30 minutes.

My point regarding rituals, habits, compounding and the exponential curve, is that when we set our minds to something, are passionate about it, and do it regularly, we can achieve massive results. When we do something, even only a little bit each day, whether it is saving five dollars, spending 30 minutes exercising, or anything else we commit to regularly, it creates an exponential curve. Initially we may find our savings doesn't grow much, or we are not getting better at what we are doing. Rest assured, with regular practice and commitment to this one task over time, the results will compound. Each day, we build on the previous day's effort or savings. Each day we become better and better. The better we become, the better we can become. The longer we spend on the task, the greater the gain. Even if the time or effort remains constant, the results exponentially increase.

Of course, as we get better at something, we tend to enjoy it more and build our confidence towards success. The more this happens, the more effort we put into it, or the more money we save. Whatever we are trying to accomplish, nothing motivates like success. Not only are we benefiting from the nature of the exponential curve, but we are becoming accustomed to this new ritual or habit. As it becomes part of our life, it is much easier to build upon. Like a runner who starts running for 30 minutes and completes a 5 km run, and slowly builds up the time and distance, the same goes with any ability, or even a savings account for that matter; it grows and grows.

When undertaking any change, I strongly suggest creating habits and rituals around what you are trying to achieve. The more you can integrate this new habit or ritual into your everyday life, the easier it is to maintain. Just don't forget, as with any regular task, stop and appreciate your progress once in a while. Celebrate your victories and your accomplishments, share them with friends and be excited and proud of how far you have come.

# Chapter 43

# Meaning, Engagement and Curiosity

*"Curiosity is the entry point to many of life's greatest sources of meaning and satisfaction: our interests, hobbies and passions"*
*Todd Kashdan*

## Find Meaning

It is well worth spending the time to find meaning in everything you do. Even the more simple or mundane tasks all have their own meaning. Whether you are cleaning the dishes in the sink, sweeping the floor, or taking out the garbage, you have the choice to see this task as boring and mundane or having meaning. The meaning may be you want to create a clean and uncluttered household for your family. The home supports them in their work or school, and helps them become the kind of person they aspire to. If you are a cleaner in a hospital, you are either just mopping the floor, or you are creating a better environment for the patients so they may recover quicker. If you are a salesman selling sunglasses, you are either just off-loading products, or you are protecting your client's eyes from the harmful rays the sun.

No matter how small or complex the task or goal is, the more meaning you can wrap around it, the more engaged you will become, and the more you will feel commitment. Meaning is one of those intangible expressions of our human emotions that we can either ignore or use to our advantage. We can decide that our life has no meaning, that we just go through from day to day without purpose, that what we do does not matter and it's only how much money we have in the bank, the size of our house, or how many possessions we have that really matters. Or we can decide that we have a purpose. That what we do from day to day has meaning. That the way we approach our day has a positive impact on other people in our lives and this in turn helps us in ways that we may not always fully understand.

Some people use religion, some people just have faith in a higher power, and some people may not believe in anything like that, yet still feel meaning and purpose in their life. If you do not have meaning, it is worth the time and energy to build meaning into your life. If you do not have meaning, then it may be worth referring back to the beginning of this book when we talk about the structure and the foundation success. Only when we fully understand our dream and our vision, and when we understand our why, will we ever start to build meaning into our life.

## Engagement

The more we engage in life, the better the outcome. By actively engaging in our day-to-day activities, we bring them meaning and interest. If we are not fully engaged in a task, it is possible that we are actually wasting our time. When we fully engage in what we are doing, we are utilizing all our mental resources towards success. The success brings future successes and so the upward spiral continues. Usually, when we are fully engaged, we are enjoying the moment more deeply. Engagement brings positivity and meaning. Often, when we are fully engaged in the task, we find a sense of flow. We become one with the task. It no longer is difficult or complex. We are able to achieve or experience what we are doing without even thinking about it. Whatever you set your mind to, I highly recommend that you engage in it fully. Make a point to be active and enthusiastic in the tasks you set your mind to. Wherever possible, get into the flow. By engaging in your activities, you are realizing your full potential. You are giving the time and energy to the task because it deserves it and you are receiving the benefit for doing so.

## Curiosity

When we are curious, we are more engaged in the world. We are always looking for new opportunities and new situations. We ask ourselves questions that challenge our assumptions. We have more certainty in our situation, because we have examined the alternatives. Less curious people on the other hand often "Rely on stereotypes, and avoid uncertainty by rejecting those who fail to conform."[172] They tend to accept everything as it is and not ask the questions needed to better understand life situations. "Curious people are able to engage for prolonged periods because the search for knowledge is in itself enjoyable."[173] This makes sense really. Think of the people that you relate to every day. Don't you notice that the more curious amongst them are the most interesting? They are fully engaged in what is happening around them and interested to explore the possibilities. "Curious people report more satisfying social interactions and relationships, and their partners describe them as interested and responsive."[174] These more satisfying social relationships flow on to better health, as we have seen previously in this book. In addition to the social relationships, it only makes sense that people who are more curious in nature are more likely to investigate alternate realities of their current situation. Ultimately, these relationships and alternate ways to deal with the world enable curious people to be healthier and live longer. One study showed that, "Those who are more curious aged 60-86 are more likely to be alive after five years, even after accounting for age, smoker status, and various diseases."[175] This statistic is very similar to another study I mention earlier in this book that shows the relationship between positive attitudes with aging and longevity. It would seem positivity and curiosity often exist hand-in-hand. Of the 24 VIA character strengths, "Curiosity was one of the most strongly linked to global life satisfaction, work satisfaction, living a pleasurable life, living an engaging life, and living a meaningful life."[176] It is easy to see the relationship between curiosity, satisfaction, engagement, and meaning.

On a personal note, my own curiosity has motivated me to travel. Driven by curiosity, I have experienced many countries and cultures across the globe. It is that wonder and sense of adventure, my curiosity about what else is out there and how other people live that has given me so much fulfillment in my life. I personally find the actions I take through my own curiosity, whether it is travel, alternate work situations, participation in clubs or social events, is what makes life so interesting. I believe without that curiosity, many of the opportunities that have come to me in life would never have occurred.

# Chapter 44

## Other Techniques

*"If not now, when?"*
*Michael Hunt*

Our final chapter lists some concepts and techniques that can be used to find happiness and success. Some have been discussed previously within this book and some concepts will be introduced.

### Podcasts and audio books

Personally, I find podcasts and audio books some of the most useful advances we have seen in technology. Utilizing these two tools, we have the ability to greatly increase our access to important information that will help us succeed. The ease of access, low-cost (or free from a library or on line) and sheer ease of consumption make them extremely useful tools. It is useful to get creative in the ways and times you can listen to them. The obvious choice is while commuting to work, school, or anything else.

Personally, I have found a much wider range of possibilities. I listen to them while cleaning the house, washing clothes and dishes, out in the garden, I even listen to them when I'm walking up to the shops. You can listen to them when you exercise or are dropping the kids off to school. There are some great books on success principles, motivation, also all sorts of inspirational topics. There are books and podcasts on almost every imaginable interest you may have. These podcasts and audio books can be easily loaded onto a smart phone, iPod, MP3 player or listened to directly from your computer. If you are not currently taking advantage of this technology, I strongly suggest that you look at all the options available.

# Visualizations

Taking advantage of visualization techniques has long been used to achieve success in many life domains. Visualizing the victory, a successful meeting, a well-presented talk, or any other success, is a great way to set yourself up for a positive result.

There has been much research in the field of visualization. Generally speaking, people who use visualizations have a higher percentage chance of success. In one 12 week study, healthy volunteers where divided into three groups. One group was trained to visualize a bending the finger exercise "mental contractions," one actually did the finger bending exercise, and one group was the control group. The group that visualized the exercise increased their finger strength by 35%. The group that actually did the exercises increased their finger strength by 53% and the control group, not surprisingly, had no change in finger strength. The researchers said, "We conclude that the mental training employed by this study enhances the cortical output signal, which drives the muscles to a higher activation level and increases strength."[177] Visualization can be a great way to set yourself up to succeed. It can allow you to "experience the situation" without having to actually be there. It can be a great training tool.

I personally feel visualization works best to open up the mind's filters to what you want to achieve, a bit like the red car example. If you are constantly thinking about a successful outcome, you open up your mind to situations and opportunities that will make it happen. If you are clear on your direction, your plans, and goals, you will automatically be thinking of these successful outcomes. This becomes a form of visualization itself. It could be argued therefore, using this logic that by having a clear vision and goals for what you want to achieve, visualization may not be required. Like all the tools, it is a matter of finding the ones that you are more comfortable with, that you can easily integrate into your daily life. If you feel visualization is one of these tools, I recommend you try it yourself. Generally speaking, for visualization to work, you should commit time to it regularly. It is not something you do once and forget about.

# Affirmations

Affirmations have being used for a long time to increase success. Affirmations can be extremely powerful when practiced regularly and when using affirmations that specifically generate emotion and passion. The more belief and desire you have for what you are affirming, the greater your chances of success. It has been shown in research that affirmations are more powerful when the mind is not sidetracked by everyday life. This could be first thing in the morning before contemplating the rest of your day. This could be also in the evening, as your mind winds down and prepares itself for rest. There are whole books and much research on effectively using affirmations.

My own personal perspective on affirmations, like visualizations, is that if you are using a solid structure for happiness and success, as discussed in this book, the use of affirmations is not as critical. When you have a clear understanding of what you are trying to achieve and clear positive planning on how you will get there, you are naturally affirming your ability to achieve your goals. You are naturally building your belief in happiness and success, not by positive thinking, but by actively planning and understanding the path to which you aspire. This clear understanding of what you must do and how you must do it provides an affirmation of your ability in itself. That said, if you feel that daily affirmations would help you better believe in your abilities, or build a better positive mindset of success, I suggest you use them with enthusiasm. Use them as often and with as much passion and emotion as you can.

# Contact with Nature

We read earlier about the benefit of contact with or views of nature. Even a small indoor plant makes a difference. Try wherever you can to increase your contact with nature. A walk in the park has great benefits, not just for your health, but also for your state of mind. In our busy life, we often neglect the walk as there are too any other things to be done and problems to solve. The reality is that sometimes a walk in the park will give your mind a chance to rest, therefore, work out a solution to a problem you have, or a better way of doing something you were doing. The time spend walking in the park may actually save you more time than what it took to take the walk. Even if it does not, the contact with nature will have other less tangible benefits. Even a picture of nature or a nature scene on your screen saver can help. Get creative with your contact with nature; if it cannot be physical, work toward a view, or at least a picture.

## Primers

There are so many ways we can prime ourselves for success. The way you prepare your physical environment and the way you communicate with others has a massive effect on your chances of success. When you fill your home and your work environment with pictures, mementos, or other objects that remind you of happy and successful times, you are setting yourself up to have more of those situations. You reinforce the positive in your life. As you see these positive reinforcers every day, your mind automatically tunes into the thoughts and emotions that come with them. These positive thoughts and emotions are what lead us towards more happiness and success, success in our work, play, vacations or whatever the object represents.

We have seen through the activation of mirror neurons in our minds that we smile when we see someone smile or see a picture of someone smiling. This is why so many advertisements have pictures of happy positive people, even if the product has nothing to do with these people. Simply by seeing them, we smile, we are more happy and positive. The same goes if you have pictures around your home or office of people smiling. Obviously, if the pictures are of yourself, your friends, family, or work colleagues, they will be much more effective in producing positive emotions. We also know that color can have a big impact. Why not ensure that there are many bright and positive colors in your environment? Cleanliness can also provide us with a sense of peace and organization. Instead of looking at that mess as simply something you need to clean up, you could look at it as an opportunity to create a more positive environment.

## Communication

When we start a conversation with a positive comment, the rest of the conversation is much more likely to be positive. Think about it, when you meet a friend or a work colleague and you immediately start complaining about someone or something, is the rest of the conversation likely to be positive or negative? How much better is the conversation when we begin with a positive comment? Always strive to begin a conversation with a positive comment, complement, or discussion about a successful outcome.

Maintaining eye contact is also critical, especially at the beginning. Think of how hard it is to maintain a positive conversation with someone when they are not looking at you. The initial few moments of a conversation makes all the difference. Aim to make eye contact with the other person from the beginning.

A smile is also very useful. You don't need to be over the top, smiling from ear to ear happy. A small smile, or at least an expression that tells the other person you are happy to be having this communication, really sets the conversation up to the more productive and successful.

Open body language is also important. When we are communicating with someone who has closed arms across their chest, we simply do not feel that they are taking in what we are saying. There has been so much study and research in the area of body language, it can become extremely confusing. A simple strategy is to keep your arms to the side and perhaps your palms facing forward. The main thing to remember is not to cross your arms or create a negative stance.

Starting a conversation on a positive note, looking the other person in the eye, the small smile and open body language can make all the difference in effective communication.

## Harness the power of If-Then

There is real power deciding, in advance, our reactions to certain situations. We can train our minds, that under a specific situation, our immediate reaction will be one that will benefit us and not just come as a surprise. This may take some time to master, yet simply by consciously having your If-Then statements prepared, you are in a much better position to react in a way that sets you up for a successful outcome. Think about situations that when they happen have a tendency to guide you in the wrong direction, make you feel negative, or you tend to take an inappropriate course of action. Write down your own If-Then statements of these situations and read and practice them often. Here are a few examples to get you thinking.

- If I walk into a room - Then I will smile and look the other people in the eye
- If it is lunchtime - Then I walk around the block before eating
- If someone says hello - Then I will look them in the eye, smile and say hello back
- If I want to eat unhealthy food - Then I will have a piece of fruit first
- If someone says something negative to me - Then I will try to understand the true meaning of the statement and to see the positive.

Harness the power of the IF - Then. You may find that this simple process can make small changes that in turn produce large results. Sometimes it is these simple primers that set us up for the correct course of action which greatly affect our chance of success and happiness.

## The early bird catches the worm.

First thing in the morning is when our minds and our bodies are most rested! We can accomplish amazing things first thing in the morning when we really put our mind to it. This could be our exercise for the day, meditation practice, completing an important task, planning our day or week, the list goes on. So often we waste the best time of the day, sorting through emails, engaged in small talk, cleaning up, etc. Many successful people get up an hour early to exercise, plan, and complete tasks. It is easy to see that if you woke up an hour early every day how much more productive your day would become. Whether you get up an hour early, 10 minutes early, or at your normal time, the most important thing is to appreciate how effective you are first thing in the morning. Limit any activities first thing in the day that are mind numbing, that do not take much motivation or creativity, or are not in line with your prime purpose for that day. There is real power in first completing your most dreaded task, your most important project, or something that is required for your own personal success that may not otherwise get done during the day.

In business, regarding money, they have a concept - pay yourself first! The idea is that you make sure you are paid before you pay all your other creditors. The reason is simple, if we pay everyone else first, we may not get paid. If we pay our self first, we generally find a way to satisfy everyone else's needs. So too with your time. So often, we spend so much time completing tasks for everyone else that we never get time to do what really matters to us. By committing each morning to doing something that will help us, whether it be exercise, planning, expanding our knowledge, or simply completing something that's been getting in our way, we set ourselves up for success. There are so many ways to get creative on this idea. The important thing is to take action and decide where you will put your priority for the first hour or so each day. If you can plan this action the day before, even better. This way, you wake up and get into it straight away with passion and enthusiasm.

## Accountability partners

As the name suggests, an accountability partner is someone who you are accountable to. Usually this is a mutual arrangement. You may meet once a week, month, or whenever you decide is suitable. You share your goals and aspirations for the coming period and you review progress from the last period. Having such an arrangement with another person has real power. In coaching, we see that one of the biggest advantages of the sessions is that the client is accountable to the coach. This is as true for sports coaching as it is for life coaching or any other personal coaching. Whilst a coach may be better trained and more experienced to support you to achieve successful outcomes, an accountability partner maybe more affordable, may involve a deeper personal connection, or simply suit you better. Whether you use an accountability partner or a coach, having someone to whom you commit is extremely important. In addition to reviewing and committing to future actions, you also have someone who you can share your successes with, no matter how small or large. This sharing of success reinforces the success and the feelings that you have associated with them. This, in turn, sets you up for future success. So find someone, whether it be a coach, work colleague, friend, or family member who you can be accountable to, and who will be supportive and encouraging through your journey.

## The Mastermind

The concept of the mastermind and mastermind group is well known in business. It is less often used to achieve personal success. The concept of the mastermind is that when two or more people, get together and share their experiences, thoughts and challenges, they create a mastermind. This mastermind is a group consciousness, or intelligence that together is more capable of finding solutions and resolving problems than any single mind. We know the concept at work when we have a brainstorm session. Everyone puts their heads together and through mutual encouragement and support, come up with solutions that the individuals could not have made on their own. A mastermind group is well structured and may meet once a week or once a month, for example. Like accountability partners, the members share their successes and challenges from a prior period and what they are planning to achieve over the next period. In addition, one or more members of the group may pose a specific challenge or obstacle that they are experiencing to the group in the hope that the mastermind, as a group, can provide an answer they had not thought of.

Mastermind groups come in all forms. Some are simply made up of a group of businessmen, usually successful, who want to capitalize on their network of other successful businessman. There are mastermind groups that are run by individuals that charge a fee to join the group. Sometimes, a less successful or experienced person may facilitate a mastermind group of businessmen above their level. They provide the facilitation services, and in return, they receive a seat at the table. Often in our personal lives we create informal mastermind groups. We talk around the kitchen table about our challenges, our successes, or problems we have. We pose a question to our group of friends, and often come up with ideas that we had not originally thought of. We know how powerful this can be. Consider for a moment if you formalized this group, if you decided to meet once a month, specifically for the purpose of supporting each other. You facilitate the discussions in a way that everyone has a fair share of the support and gets the chance to speak. Imagine the power of this group when you can prepare your questions or problems in advance, knowing that you will have a chance to access this mastermind. There can be real power in having a set time and group to do this work with.

If you are in a situation in your business or personal life where you feel access to a mastermind would be beneficial, it may be worth seeking out a mastermind group in your area or starting one of your own.

# Enthusiasm

I talk a lot about positivity and enthusiasm in this book. If you want to build your enthusiasm, you simply need to find something you are enthusiastic about! Find something that utilizes your strengths, and maintains your interest so much so that you look forward to it. If you find your life lacks enthusiasm, you should seriously look at where you are spending your time. Are you spending too much time watching television, surfing the net, not challenging yourself, doing things you don't want to be doing? Another killer of enthusiasm is perspective. Even if you are locked into a job that gives you little satisfaction or interest, you may still, with some creativity, build in meaning. This, in turn, will lead to enthusiasm. If you spend your life mopping floors, make them shine. Think of what else you can do during your day that will add value to your clients, co-workers, or family. Building enthusiasm is not getting away with doing as little work as possible. Enthusiastic people do not try to get out of as much work or commitment as they can. Enthusiastic people challenge themselves, try something new, communicate with other people, and are always looking for interesting or exciting way to spend their time. Another great way to build your enthusiasm is to ensure that you are using your signature strengths. If you lack enthusiasm in your day-to-day activities, look to see if you are using your signature strengths often. If you are not using your strengths, not doing what you're good at, look at ways you can re-craft your day to do so. There is nothing better to build enthusiasm than to be doing what you love and doing it well.

# Faith

Build your faith. It is extremely beneficial to have faith in something. It could be religion, it could be in your mission for personal growth, it could be in other people. Faith is often assumed to be all about religion. Faith in a religion has been proven to have many beneficial effects; it is good for the community and allows you to be in touch with a great source of power or knowledge. Faith, however, has many different flavors. Generally speaking, if you would like faith to work for you within your life, you should find faith in a power greater than yourself. This could be of a spiritual nature, or it could be something more down-to-earth, such as in the local Rotary club, sports club, or other community organization. The real power in having faith in something bigger than yourself is that it allows you to have a broader perspective on life. You become less self-centered as you build your faith. Your life becomes less just about you and more part of a bigger picture. This can only have positive ramifications within your life. If you are living a life without faith in anything, I recommend you begin a search for something you can put your faith in. If what you are trying now is not working for you, perhaps it's time to look at something else. Like everything, the more passion, emotion, and belief in the thing you are searching for, or have found, the easier it is to have faith. Everyone's faith is very personal to themselves. For this reason, I do not recommend a specific path. I only suggest that the more faith you have in something larger than yourself, the better your life will become.

## Compassion

*"If you want others to be happy, practice compassion; if you want to be happy, practice compassion." Dalai Lama*

Compassionate people are happier. As you build your positivity and your gratitude, you will naturally become more compassionate. Meditation and mindfulness have also been shown to build compassion. Simply by noticing the world around you, the people you see, you naturally lean towards compassion. The more you grow and develop yourself, the better in touch with your inner self you are, the more compassion you develop.

Researchers at the Center for Investigating Healthy Minds at the Waisman Center of the University of Wisconsin-Madison show that adults can be trained to be more compassionate. They used an ancient Buddhist technique, compassion meditation, and received great results. If you really want to build your compassion, you can try such techniques. Alternately, by following the structure to happiness and success, utilizing your strengths and building positive relationships, plus using the key tools to underpin this structure, you will be more in line with your true self. The better we understand ourselves and the true nature of the world around us, the happier and the more compassionate we become.

## Emotions come first

Whenever we want to change anything, it starts with emotion. The part of our brain that controls emotion is where the neurons first light up before we complete any activity. Emotions prompt us to make decisions. Emotions are also what drive us into motion, into action. Emotion came from the word "*esmovoir*," to set in motion. Without emotion, we don't have motion. As discussed previously in this book, the word motivation came from movement. We get motivation from our motion. We get motivation from our emotion. With everything we do, we should build in as much emotion as we can. It's that feeling, the passion, the drive that comes from something that we are emotionally attached to that gets us moving. The bigger the challenge, the more emotion we should have around accomplishing that challenge.

## Getting Help

There is a lot more help out there than you realize. Help can be available through friends, family, work colleagues, or social groups. You would be amazed how many people you know will support you in your journey, some of whom initially may not be obvious. With some of your more complex challenges, especially removing roadblocks, there is a vast array of groups and organizations that are available to assist. Many of these groups are self-supporting or funded by government, local councils, or community groups. The programs that are on offer for specific issues can be extremely effective.

One of the biggest roadblocks that people encounter is the willingness to seek outside assistance. Often, once the initial fear of reaching out for assistance is overcome, the journey is a lot easier than ever imagined. Help can also come from other resources such as libraries, websites, or podcasts.

Think of what you like, and what inspires and interests you. Are there resources available that will engage you or empower you through your journey of change?

## Support structure

With any change in your life, in addition to initial help, it is crucial to have ongoing support. This support may come from friends and family, community groups, or professional support. The type of support an individual needs in order to create a fulfilling, happy, and successful life is very personal to that person. The type of support needs to work for you. Critically, you need to ensure that you do have an ongoing support structure in place. You may use an accountability partner, a mastermind group, a therapist, or a coach. Of course, I highly recommend the use of a coach in any forward thinking process of change. A coach can provide accountability, structure, encouragement, and support. Coaching can vary from one-on-one, face-to-face weekly sessions, monthly catch ups, group sessions, the list goes on. Some people prefer coaching via phone, email, or Skype.

The key to any support structure is to find something that works for you. Whilst going it alone may seem a practical and good idea at first, it can be difficult to maintain the momentum. This is not to say that many people do not use this technique. I really recommend if you are coaching yourself, however, to ensure you are always reading new ideas and thoughts on self-development. You could listen to podcasts, watch videos, or whatever else works for you.

If you enlist a coach, join a good group, or club that is focused towards growth and change, make sure it works for you. If it is not working, try something else. Importantly, you should be active and engaged in your support structure whatever it may be. In addition, if you need additional assistance or support outside this structure, you should seek it.

I have clients who have me as a coach and who also have a therapist. I have clients who also undertake self-development courses, watch videos, and read books on the subject in which they're developing. A multi-facet approach to your own development does not mean your support structure is not good enough; it shows that you are passionate, intelligent, and actively working towards the best possible result that you can find. If you have multiple support structures, let everyone know what's going on. You should be proud that you are able to manage this multi-pronged approach. You should be proud of the dedication and commitment you have to maintain a solid support structure that will give you the maximum chance of achieving your goals.

## Chapter 45

# Conclusion

*"Most action is based on redemption and revenge, and that's a formula. Moby Dick was formula. It's how you get to the conclusion that makes it interesting"*
*Sylvester Stallone*

Thank you for your time spent reading this book. I hope you have gained valuable insight and knowledge that will support you to live a happy, more fulfilling, and successful life. Remember that change and happiness is a journey. We spent a lot of time talking about the ultimate dream and your goals. We have looked at ways on how to achieve happiness and success. Ultimately, however, it is not achieving your goals that will give you the maximum benefit. It is the meaning and purpose you feel, your perspective and attitude towards your day, and your journey that will give you the most satisfaction and happiness.

Living a life full of passion and enthusiasm, using our creativity and having a deep sense of what we are doing, makes a difference to us and others; this is success. Success is experiencing happiness, joy, and excitement. Success is doing what you love and doing it well. Success is enjoying positive relationships in your life. Money and other possessions are only tools that we can use to support us on this journey of life. They are not the ultimate goal. The goal is the journey, the experiences, the relationships, and the satisfaction we gain by living a great life. Our goal is to grow, to learn, and to be our best selves.

Again, I thank you for your time. By reading this book, you have helped me on my journey. You have helped me find my meaning and purpose. You have encouraged me to continue on my journey, to coach, train, mentor, and encourage others to be the best that they can be.

If you got something from this book, if it has changed you in a positive way, please share it or tell others about it. Contact me if you have any questions or want to know more. Come to one of my workshops or other training events. Take advantage of some one-on-one coaching. Most of all, verify your vision, go for your goals, prepare your plans, and take action. Build your motivation through movement. Find your satisf**action**.

# References

1   Edwin, A., Locke and Gary, P., Latham R H. New Directions in Goal-Setting Theory. Smith School of Business, University of Maryland, and Rotman School of Management, University of Toronto.

2   Edwin, A.,. Locke and Gary, P., Latham R., H. New Directions in Goal-Setting Theory. Smith School of Business, University of Maryland, and Rotman School of Management, University of Toronto.

3   Latham G.P, Brown T C (in press). The effect of learning, distal, and proximal goals on MBA self-efficacy and satisfaction. Applied Psychology: An International Review.

4   Fred C Lunenburg, Sam Houston. 2001. International Journal of Management, Business and Administration, Volume 15, Number 1, Goal-Setting Theory of Motivation State University.

5   Edwin A., Locke and Gary P Latham R H. New Directions in Goal-Setting Theory, Smith School of Business, University of Maryland, and Rotman School of Management, University of Toronto.

6   Baum, J. R, & Locke E A. (2004). The relationship of entrepreneurial traits, skill, and motivation to subsequent venture growth. Journal of Applied Psychology, 89, 587598.

7   Kristof-Brown, A. L., & Stevens, C. K. (2001). Goal congruence in project teams: Does the fit between members' personal mastery and performance goals matter?

8   Locke, E. A., & Latham, G. P. (1984). Goal setting: A motivational technique that works! Englewood Cliffs, NJ: Prentice Hall.

9   Latham, G. P., & Kinne, S. B. (1974). Improving job performance through training in goal setting. Journal of Applied Psychology, 59, 187191.

10  Latham, G. P., & Baldes, J. (1975). The "practical significance" of Locke's theory of goal setting. Journal of Applied Psychology, 60, 122124.

11  Latham, G. P., & Yukl, G. A. (1975). Assigned versus participative goal setting with educated and uneducated wood workers. Journal of Applied Psychology, 60, 299 302.

12  Terpstra, D. E., & Rozell, E. J. (1994). The relationship of goal setting to organizational profitability. Group and Organization Management, 19, 285294.

13  Little, B. R., Salmela-Aro, K., & Phillips, S. D. (2007). Personal project pursuit. Goals, action, and human flourishing. Lawrence Erlbaum Associates.

14  Little, B. R., & Chambers, N. (2000). Analyse des projets personnels: un cadre intégratif pour la psychologie clinique et le counseling. Revue québécoise de psychologie, *21*, 153-189.

15  Ryan, R. M., & Deci, E. L. (2000). Self-determination theory and the facilitation of intrinsic motivation, social development, and well-being. American Psychologist, *55*(1), 68-78.

16  Deci, E. L., & Ryan, R. M. (2008). Self-determination theory: A macrotheory of human motivation, development, and health. *Canadian Psychology, 49*(3), 182-185. http://dx.doi.org/10.1037/a0012801

17  Sheldon, K. M., & Kasser, T. (2001). Goals, congruence, and positive well-being: New empirical support for humanistic theories. *Journal of Humanistic Psychology, 41*(1), 30-50.

18  Seligman, M.E.P., Steen, T., Park, N. & Peterson, C.(2005). Positive psychology progress: Empirical validation of interventions. American Psychologist, 60, 410–421.

19  Peterson, C., Park., N. & Seligman (2006). Greater strengths of character and recovery from illness. Journal of Positive Psychology, *1*, 17–26.

20  Linley, P.A. (2008c). Psychotherapy as strength-spotting. The Psychotherapist, *39*, 4–5.

21  Govindji, R. & Linley, P.A. (2007). Strengths use, selfconcordance and well-being: Implications for strengths coaching and coaching psychologists. International Coaching Psychology Review, *2*(2), 143–153.

22  Biswas-Diener, R. (2009). Coaching as a positive intervention. Journal of Clinical Psychology, *65*, 544–553

23  P. Alex Linley, Karina M. Nielsen, Raphael Gillett & Robert Biswas-Diener Using signature strengths in pursuit of goals: Effects on goal progress, need satisfaction, and well-being, and implications for coaching psychologists

24  Sonja Lyubomirsky The Benefits of Frequent Positive Affect: Does Happiness Lead to Success?, University of California, Riverside

25  Sonja Lyubomirsky, Laura King, University of California, Riverside University of Missouri--Columbia; Ed Diener, University of Illinois at UrbanaChampaign and The Gallup Organization. The Benefits of Frequent Positive Affect: Does Happiness Lead to Success?

26  *Elliot, A. J., & Thrash, T. M. (2002). Approach–avoidance motivation in personality: Approach and avoidance temperaments and goals. Journal of Personality and Social Psychology, *82*, 804–818.

27  Cantor et al., 1991;Carver & Scheier, 1998; Clore, Wyer, Dienes, Gasper, & Isbell, 2001

28  Fredrickson, B. L., & Levenson, R. W. (1998). Positive emotions speed recovery from the cardiovascular sequelae of negative emotions. Cognition and Emotion, *12*, 191–220.

29  Fredrickson, B. L., & Levenson, R. W. (1998). Positive emotions speed recovery from the cardiovascular sequelae of negative emotions. Cognition and Emotion, *12,* 191–220.

30  Sonja Lyubomirsky The Benefits of Frequent Positive Affect: Does Happiness Lead to Success?, University of California, Riverside

31  Frisch, M. B., Clark, M. P., Rouse, S. V., Rudd, M. D., Paweleck, J. K. Greenstone, A., et al. (2004). Predictive and treatment validity of life satisfaction and the Quality of Life Inventory. *Assessment, 10,* 1–13.

32  Staw, B. M., Sutton, R. I., & Pelled, L. H. (1994). Employee positive emotion and favorable outcomes at the workplace. *Organization Science, 5,* 51–71.

33  Wright, T. A., & Cropanzano, R. (2000). Psychological well-being and job satisfaction as predictors of job performance. Journal of Occupational Health Psychology, *5,* 84–94.

34  Totterdell, P. (2000). Catching moods and hitting runs: Mood linkage and subjective performance in professional sports teams. Journal of Applied Psychology, *83,* 848–859.

35  *George, J. M. (1995). Leader positive mood and group performance: The case of customer service. *Journal of Applied Social Psychology, 25,* 778–795.

36  Foster, J. B., Hebl, M. R., West, M., & Dawson, J. (2004, April). Setting the tone for organizational success: The impact of CEO affect on organizational climate and firm-level outcomes. Paper presented at the 17th annual meeting of the Society for Industrial and Organizational Psychology, Toronto, Ontario, Canada.

37  Pritzker, M. A. (2002). The relationship among CEO dispositional attributes, transformational leadership behaviors and performance effectiveness. Dissertation Abstracts International, *62*(12-B), 6008. (UMI No. AAI3035464)

38  Wright, T. A., & Staw, B. M. (1999). Affect and favorable work outcomes: Two longitudinal tests of the happy—Productive worker thesis. Journal of Organizational Behavior, *20,* 1–23.

39  Barsade, S. G., Ward, A. J., Turner, J. D. F., & Sonnenfeld, J. A. (2000). To your heart's content: A model of affective diversity in top management teams. Administrative Science Quarterly, *45,* 802–836.

40  Cacha, F. B. (1976). Figural creativity, personality, and peer nominations of pre-adolescents. Gifted Child Quarterly, *20,* 187–195

41  Lucas, R. E., Diener, E., Grob, A., Suh, E. M., & Shao, L. (2000). Cross-cultural evidence for the fundamental features of extraversion. Journal of Personality and Social Psychology, *79,* 452–468.

42  Kashdan, T. B., Rose, P., & Fincham, F. D. (2004). Curiosity and exploration: Facilitating positive subjective experiences and personal growth opportunities. Journal of Personality Assessment, *82,* 291–305.

43  Fredrickson, B. L. (1998). What good are positive emotions? Review of General Psychology, *2*, 300–319.

44  Diener, E., & Fujita, F. (1995). Resources, personal strivings, and subjective well-being: A nomothetic and idiographic approach. Journal of Personality and Social Psychology, *68*, 926–935.

45  Headey, B., & Veenhoven, R. (1989). Does happiness induce a rosy outlook? In R. Veenhoven (Ed.), How harmful is happiness? Consequences of enjoying life or not (pp. 106–127). Rotterdam, the Netherlands: Universitaire Pers Rotterdam.

46  Gottman, J. M., & Levenson, R. W. (1999). What predicts change in marital interaction over time? A study of alternative medicine. Family Process, *38*, 143–158.

47  Diener, E., Wolsic, B., & Fujita, F. (1995). Physical attractiveness and subjective well-being. Journal of Personality and Social Psychology, 69, 120–129.

48  Schimmack, U., Oishi, S., Furr, R. M., & Funder, D. C. (2004). Personality and life satisfaction: A facet-level analysis. Personality and Social Psychology Bulletin, *30*, 1062–1075.

49  Rimland, B. (1982). The altruism paradox. Psychological Reports, *51*, 521–522.

50  Diener, E., & Fujita, F. (1995). Resources, personal strivings, and subjective well-being: A nomothetic and idiographic approach. Journal of Personality and Social Psychology, 68, 926–935.

51  Feingold, A. (1983). Happiness, unselfishness, and popularity. *Journal of Psychology, 115,* 3–5.

52  *Rigby, K., & Slee, P. T. (1993). Dimensions of interpersonal relation among Australian children and implications for psychological wellbeing. Journal of Social Psychology, *133*, 33–42.

53  Staw, B. M., Sutton, R. I., & Pelled, L. H. (1994). Employee positive emotion and favorable outcomes at the workplace. Organization Science,5, 51–71.

54  Diener, E., & Seligman, M. E. P. (2002). Very happy people. Psychological Science, 13, 81–84.

55  Wilson, W. (1967). Correlates of avowed happiness. Psychological Bulletin, 67, 294–306.

56  Pinquart, M., & So¨rensen, S. (2000). Influences of socioeconomic status, social network, and competence on subjective well-being in later life: A meta-analysis. Psychology and Aging, 15, 187–224.

57  Graham, C., Eggers, A., & Sukhtankar, S. (in press). Does happiness pay? An exploration based on panel data from Russia. Journal of Economic Behaviour and Organization.

58  Achat, H., Kawachi, I., Spiro, A., III, DeMolles, D. A., & Sparrow, D. (2000). Optimism and depression as predictors of physical and mental health functioning: The Normative Aging Study. Annals of Behavioral Medicine, 22, 127–130.

59  Sonja Lyubomirsky The Benefits of Frequent Positive Affect: Does Happiness Lead to Success? University of California, Riverside

60  Watson, D. (1988). Intraindividual and interindividual analyses of positive and negative affect: Their relation to health complaints, perceived stress, and daily activities. Journal of Personality and Social Psychology,54, 1020–1030.

61  Lox, C. L., Burns, S. P., Treasure, D. C., & Wasley, D. A. (1999). Physical and psychological predictors of exercise dosage in healthy adults. Medicine and Science in Sports and Exercise, 31, 1060–1064.

62  Alden, A. L., Dale, J. A., & DeGood, D. E. (2001). Interactive effects of the affect quality and directional focus of mental imagery on pain analgesia. Applied Psychophysiology and Biofeedback, 26, 117–126.

63  Smith, T. W., Ruiz, J. M., & Uchino, B. N. (2004). Mental activation of supportive ties, hostility, and cardiovascular reactivity to laboratory stress in young men and women. Health Psychology, 23, 476–485.

64  Cohen, S., Doyle, W. J., Turner, R. B., Alper, C. M., & Skoner, D. P. (2003). Emotional style and susceptibility to the common cold. Psychosomatic Medicine, 65, 652–657.

65  Vitaliano, P. P., Scanlan, J. M., Ochs, H. D., Syrjala, K., Siegler, I. C., & Snyder, E. A. (1998). Psychosocial stress moderates the relationship of cancer history with natural killer cell activity. Annals of Behavioral Medicine, 20, 199–208.

66  Graham, C., Eggers, A., & Sukhtankar, S. (in press). Does happiness pay? An exploration based on panel data from Russia. Journal of Economic Behaviour and Organization.

67  Ostir, G. V., Markides, K. S., Peek, M. K., & Goodwin, J. S. (2001). The association between emotional well-being and the incidence of stroke in older adults. Psychosomatic Medicine, 63, 210–215.

68  Smith, A. M., Stuart, M. J., Wiese-Bjornstal, D. M., & Gunnon, C. (1997). Predictors of injury in ice hockey players: A multivariate, multidisciplinary approach. American Journal of Sports Medicine, 25, 500–507.

69  Kubzansky, L. D., Sparrow, D., Vokonas, P., & Kawachi, I. (2001). Is the glass half empty or half full? A prospective study of optimism and coronary heart disease in the normative aging study. Psychosomatic Medicine, 63, 910–916.

70  *Scheier, M. F., Matthews, K. A., Owens, J. F., Magovern, G. J., Lefebvre, R. C., Abbott, R., A., et al. (1989). Dispositional optimism and recovery from coronary artery bypass surgery: The beneficial effects on physical and psychological well-being. Journal of Personality and Social Psychology, 57, 1024–1040.

71  Fitzgerald, T. E., Prochaska, J. O., & Pransky, G. S. (2000). Health risk reduction and functional restoration following coronary revascularization: A prospective investigation using dynamic stage typology clustering. International Journal of Rehabilitation and Health, 5, 99–116.

72 Kirkcaldy, B., & Furnham, A. (2000). Positive affectivity, psychological well-being, accident- and traffic-deaths and suicide: An international comparison. Studia Psychologica, 42, 97–104.

73 Koivumaa-Honkanen, H., Honkanen, R., Koskenvuo, M., Viinamaeki, H., & Kaprio, J. (2002). Life satisfaction as a predictor of fatal injury in a 20-year follow-up. Acta Psychiatrica Scandinavica, 105, 444–450.

74 Levy, S. M., Lee, J., Bagley, C., & Lippman, M. (1988). Survival hazard analysis in first recurrent breast cancer patients: Seven-year follow-up. Psychosomatic Medicine, 50, 520–528.

75 *Krause, J. S., Sternberg, M., Lottes, S., & Maides, J. (1997). Mortality after spinal cord injury: An 11-year prospective study. Archives of Physical Medicine and Rehabilitation, 78, 815 821.

76 Levy, B. R., Slade, M. D., Kunkel, S. R., & Kasl, S. V. (2002). Longevity increased by positive self-perceptions of aging. Journal of Personality and Social Psychology, 83, 261–270

77 Zuckerman, D. M., Kasl, S. V., & Ostfeld, A. M. (1984). Psychosocial predictors of mortality among the elderly poor. The role of religion, well-being, and social contacts. American Journal of Epidemiology, 119, 410–423.

78 Zuckerman, D. M., Kasl, S. V., & Ostfeld, A. M. (1984). Psychosocial predictors of mortality among the elderly poor. The role of religion, well-being, and social contacts. American Journal of Epidemiology, 119, 410–423.

79 Deeg, D. J. H., & Van Zonneveld, R. J. (1989). Does happiness lengthen life? The prediction of longevity in the elderly. In R. Veenhoven (Ed.), How harmful is happiness? Consequences of enjoying life or not (pp. 29–34). Rotterdam, the Netherlands: Universitaire Pers Rotterdam.

80 Danner, D. D., Snowdon, D. A., & Friesen, W. V. (2001). Positive emotions in early life and longevity: Findings from the nun study. Journal of Personality and Social Psychology, 80, 804–813.

81 Maruta, T., Colligan, R. C., Malinchoc, M., & Offord, K. P. (2000). Optimists vs. pessimists: Survival rate among medical patients over a 30-year period. Mayo Clinic Proceedings, 75, 140–143.

82 Kubzansky, L. D., Sparrow, D., Vokonas, P., & Kawachi, I. (2001). Is the glass half empty or half full? A prospective study of optimism and coronary heart disease in the normative aging study. Psychosomatic Medicine, 63, 910–916.

83 Barbara L. Fredrickson, 2001 March, The Role of Positive Emotions in Positive Psychology:-The Broaden-and-Build Theory of Positive Emotions University of Michigan;

84 Barbara L. Fredrickson and Marcial F. Losada. Positive Affect and the Complex Dynamics of Human Flourishing

85 Fredrickson BL, Joiner T, Positive emotions trigger upward spirals toward emotional well-being. Psychol Sci. 2002 Mar; 13(2):172-5.

86  Fredrickson BL, Branigan C. Positive emotions broaden the scope of attention and thought-action repertoires. Cogn Emot. 2005 May 1; 19(3):313-332

87  Burns AB, Brown JS, Sachs-Ericsson N, Plant EA, Curtis JT, Fredrickson BL, et al. Upward spirals of positive emotion and coping: Replication, extension, and initial exploration of neurochemical substrates. Personality and Individual Differences. 2008; 44:360–370.

88  Eric L. Garland, Barbara Fredrickson, Ann, M. Kring, David P. Johnson, Piper S. Meyer and David L. Penn. Upward Spirals of Positive Emotions Counter Downward Spirals of Negativity: Insights from the Broaden-and-Build Theory and Affective Neuroscience on The Treatment of Emotion Dysfunctions and Deficits in Psychopathology.

89  Fredrickson BL, Branigan C. Positive emotions broaden the scope of attention and thought-action repertoires. Cognition and Emotion. 2005; 19(3):313–332

90  Lazarus, R. Emotion and adaptation. New York: Oxford University Press; 1991.

91  Eric L. Garland, Barbara Fredrickson, Ann, M. Kring, David P. Johnson, Piper S. Meyer and David L. Penn. Upward Spirals of Positive Emotions Counter Downward Spirals of Negativity: Insights from the Broaden-and-Build Theory and Affective Neuroscience on The Treatment of Emotion Dysfunctions and Deficits in Psychopathology.

92  Fredrickson BL, Branigan C. Positive emotions broaden the scope of attention and thought-action repertoires. Cognition and Emotion. 2005; 19(3):313–332.

93  Wadlinger HA, Isaacowitz DM. Positive mood broadens visual attention to positive stimuli. Motivation and Emotion. 2006; 30(1):87–99. [PubMed: 20431711]

94  Schmitz TW, De Rosa E, Anderson AK. Opposing influences of affective state valence on visual cortical encoding. Journal of Neuroscience. 2009; 29(22):7199–7207. [PubMed: 19494142]

95  Fredrickson BL, Branigan C. Positive emotions broaden the scope of attention and thought-action repertoires. Cognition and Emotion. 2005; 19(3):313–332.

96  Rowe G, Hirsh JB, Anderson AK. Positive affect increases the breadth of attentional selection. Proceedings of the National Academy of Sciences USA. 2007; 104(1):383–388

97  Kahn BE, Isen AM. The influence of positive affect on variety seeking among safe, enjoyable products. Journal of Consumer Research. 1993; 20(2):257–270

98  Langer, E.J. (1997) The Power of Mindful Learning. Reading, MA: Addison-Wesley.

99  Kriger, M.P. and Hanson, B.J. (1999) A value-based paradigm for creating truly healthy organizations. Journal of Organizational Change Management, 12(4), 302-17.

100 Shefy, E. and Sadler-Smith, E. (2006) Applying holistic principles in management development. Journal of Management Development, 25(4), 36885.

101 Adams, H.L. (2007) Mindful use as a link between social capital and organizational learning: An empirical test of the antecedents and consequences

of two new constructs. Dissertation. Abstracts International, Section A: Humanities and Social Sciences, 67(11-A), 4243.

102 Walach, H., Nord, E., and Zier, C. (2007) Mindfulness-based stress reduction as a method for personnel development: A pilot evaluation. International Journal of Stress Management, 14(2), 188-98.

103 Williams, V., Ciarrochi, J., and Deane, F.P. (2010) On being mindful, emotionally aware, and more resilient: Longitudinal pilot study of police recruits. Australian Psychologist, 45(4), 27482.

104 Williams, V., Ciarrochi, J., and Deane, F.P. (2010) On being mindful, emotionally aware, and more resilient: Longitudinal pilot study of police recruits. Australian Psychologist, 45(4), 27482.

105 Marrs, P.C. (2007) The enactment of fear in conversations-gone-bad at work. Dissertation Abstracts, International Section A: Humanities and Social Sciences, 68(6-A), 2545.

106 Ivtzan, I., Gardner, H. E., & Smailova, Z., (2011). Mindfulness meditation and curiosity: The contributing factors to wellbeing and the process of closing the self-discrepancy gap. International Journal of Wellbeing, 1(3), 316-327. doi:10.5502/ijw.v1i3.2 University College London.

107 Grégoire S, Bouffard T, Vezeau C. (2012). Personal goal setting as mediator of the relationship between mindfulness and wellbeing. International Journal of Wellbeing, 2(3), 236-250. doi:10.5502/ijw.v2.i3.5

108 Eric L. Garland, Barbara Fredrickson, Ann, M. Kring, David P. Johnson, Piper S. Meyer and David L. Penn Upward Spirals of Positive Emotions Counter Downward Spirals of Negativity Insights from the Broaden-and-Build Theory and Affective Neuroscience on The Treatment of Emotion Dysfunctions and Deficits in Psychopathology.

109 Antoine Lutz, Lawrence L Greischar, Nancy B Rawlings, Matthieu Ricard, and Richard J. Davidson. Long-term meditators self-induce high-amplitude gamma synchrony during mental practice. Keck Laboratory for Functional Brain Imaging and Behavior, Waisman Center, and Laboratory for Affective Neuroscience, Department.

110 Barbara L. Fredrickson, Michael A. Cohn, Kimberly A. Coffey, Jolynn Pek, and Sandra M. Finkel. Open Hearts Build Lives: Positive Emotions, Induced Through Loving-Kindness Meditation, Build Consequential Personal Resources

111 Weiss, H. M., Nicholas, J. P., & Daus, C. S. (1999). An examination of the joint effects of affective experiences and job beliefs on job satisfaction and variations in affective experiences over time. Organizational Behavior and Human Decision Processes, 78, 1–24.

112 Graef, R., Csikszentmihalyi, M., & Gianinno, S. M. (1983). Measuring intrinsic motivation in everyday life. Leisure Studies, 2, 155–168.

113 Hektner, J. M. (1997). Exploring optimal personality development: A longitudinal study of adolescents. Dissertation Abstracts International, 57(11B), 7249. (UMI No. AAM9711187)

114 Forgas, J. P. (1989). Mood effects on decision making strategies. Australian Journal of Psychology, 41, 197–214.

115 *Jundt, D., & Hinsz, V. B. (2001, May). Are happier workers more productive workers? The impact of mood on self-set goals, self-efficacy, and task performance. Paper presented at the annual meeting of the Midwestern Psychological Association, Chicago.

116 Estrada, C. A., Isen, A. M., & Young, M. J. (1997). Positive affect facilitates integration of information and decreases anchoring in reasoning among physicians. Organizational Behavior and Human Decision Processes, 72, 117–135.

117 Isen, A. M., & Means, B. (1983). The influence of positive affect on decision-making strategy. Social Cognition, 2, 18–31.

118 Erez, A., & Isen, A. M. (2002). The influence of positive affect on the components of expectancy motivation. Journal of Applied Psychology, 87, 1055–1067.

119 Isen, A. M. (2000). Positive affect and decision making. In M. Lewis & J. M. Haviland-Jones (Eds.), Handbook of emotions (2nd ed., pp. 417– 435). New York: Guilford Press.

120 Boldero, J., & Francis, J. (2000). The relation between self discrepancies and emotion: The moderating roles of self-guide importance, location relevance, and social self-domain centrality. Journal of Personality and Social Psychology, 78, 38-52. http://dx.doi.org/10.1037/0022-3514.78.1.38

121 Ivtzan, I., Gardner, H. E., & Smailova, Z. (2011). Mindfulness meditation and curiosity: The contributing factors to wellbeing and the process of closing the self-discrepancy gap. International Journal of Wellbeing, 1(3), 316-327. doi:10.5502/ijw.v1i3.2

122 Moore, A., & Malinowski, P. (2009). Meditation, mindfulness and cognitive flexibility. Consciousness and Cognition, 18(1), 176-186. http://dx.doi.org/10.1016/j.concog.2008.12.008

123 As defined by http://www.medicinenet.com/

124 Turlejski K, Djavadian R. Life-long stability of neurons: a century of research on neurogenesis, neuronal death and neuron quantification in adult CNS. Progress in Brain Research. 2002; 136:39–65. [PubMed: 12143397]

125 Eric L. Garland, Barbara Fredrickson, Ann, M. Kring, David P. Johnson, Piper S. Meyer and David L. Penn. Upward Spirals of Positive Emotions Counter Downward Spirals of Negativity: Insights from the Broaden-and-Build Theory and Affective Neuroscience on The Treatment of Emotion Dysfunctions and Deficits in Psychopathology.

126 Cohn MA, Fredrickson BL. In search of durable positive psychology interventions: Predictors and consequences of long-term positive behavior change. 2010 Manuscript under review

127 Sourya Acharya and Samarth Shukla. Mirror neurons: Enigma of the metaphysical modular brain Page 1 - Jul-Dec 2012

128 Richins, M.L. and S. Dawson: 1992, A consumer values orientation for materialism and its measurement: Scale development and validation, Journal of Consumer Research 19, pp. 303–316.

129 Wikipedia

130 Maslow, A. (1954). Motivation and personality. New York, NY: Harper. pp. 91.

131 Kasser, T.: 2002, The High Price of Materialism (The MIT Press, Cambridge, MA).

132 Richins, M.L. and S. Dawson: 1992, A consumer values orientation for materialism and its measurement: Scale development and validation, Journal of Consumer Research 19, pp. 303–316.

133 Belk, R.W.: 1985, Materialism: Trait aspects of living in the material world, Journal of Consumer Research 12, pp. 265–280.

134 Kasser, T., R.M. Ryan, C.E. Couchman and K.M. Sheldon: 2004, Materialistic values: Their causes and consequences, in T. Kasser and A.D. Kanner (eds), Psychology and Consumer Culture: The struggle for a Good Life in a Materialistic World (American Psychological Association, Washington, DC), pp. 11–28.

135 Richins, M.L. and S. Dawson: 1992, A consumer values orientation for materialism and its measurement: Scale development and validation, Journal of Consumer Research 19, pp. 303–316.

136 Emily L Polak, Michael E McCullough. Journal of Happiness Studies (2006) 7:343–360. Is Gratitude an alternative to Materialism?

137 Kasser, T.: 2002, The High Price of Materialism. The MIT Press, Cambridge, MA.

138 Emily L Polak, Michael E McCullough. Journal of Happiness Studies (2006) 7:343–360. Is Gratitude an alternative to Materialism?

139 Kasser, T.: 2004, Materialistic Desires Scale. Unpublished questionnaire. Knox College, Galesburg, IL.

140 Rindfleisch, A., J.E. Burroughs and F. Denton: 1997, Family structure, materialism, and compulsive consumption, Journal of Consumer Research 23, pp. 312–325.

141 Abramson, P.R. and R. Inglehart: 1995, Value Change in Global Perspective University of Michigan Press, Ann Arbor.

142 Van Kampen, 2003.

143 Kasser, T.: 2002, The High Price of Materialism. The MIT Press, Cambridge, MA.

144 Leaf Van Boven, University of Colorado at Boulder, Thomas Gilovich, Cornell University. Journal of Personality and Social Psychology. To Do or to Have? That Is the Question.

145 Leaf Van Boven, University of Colorado at Boulder, Thomas Gilovich, Cornell University. Journal of Personality and Social Psychology. To Do or to Have? That Is the Question.

146 Wikipedia

147 Daniel J. Simons, Professor of Psychology. Division: Visual Cognition & Human Performance.

148 [Chabris, C. F., & Simons, D. J. (2010). See http://www.theinvisiblegorilla.com/

149 T. Singh. www.gurbani.org

150 Ekman, P., Davidson, R. J., Ricard, M. & Wallace, B. A. (2005). Buddhist and Psychological Perspectives on Emotions and Well-Being. Current Directions in Psychological Science, 14, 59-63.

151 The Joy of Living - (2007, p. 32)

152 Ricard, M. (2006). Happiness: A Guide to Developing Life's Most Important Skill. Boston: Little, Brown and Co.

153 Kasser, T. (2008). ‚Can Buddhism and Consumerism Harmonize? A Review of the Psychological Evidence. International Conference on Buddhism in the Age of Consumerism, Mahidol University, Bangkok, 1-3 December 2008.

154 Kasser, T. (2002). The High Price of Materialism. Cambridge, MA: MIT Press.

155 Kasser T, Vansteenkiste M, & Deckop J. R. (2006). The Ethical Problems of a Materialistic Values Orientation for Businesses (and Some Suggestions for Alternatives). In J. R. Deckop (ed.), Human Resource Management Ethics (pp. 283-306). Greenwich, CT: Information Age Publishing, Inc.

156 Kasser, T. (2006). Materialism and its Alternatives. In M. Csikszentmihály & I. S. Csikszentmihály (eds.), A Life Worth Living: Contributions to Positive Psychology (pp. 200-214). Oxford: Oxford University Press

157 Ricard, M. (2011). The Dalai Lama: Happiness from within. International Journal of Wellbeing, 1 (2), 274- 290. doi:10.5502/ijw.v1i2.9

158 Ricard, M. (2010). Why Meditate? Working with Thoughts and Emotions. New York: Hay House.

159 Ricard, M. (2011). The Dalai Lama: Happiness from within. International Journal of Wellbeing, 1 (2), 274- 290. doi:10.5502/ijw.v1i2.9

160 Ricard, M. (2011). The Dalai Lama: Happiness from within. International Journal of Wellbeing, 1 (2), 274- 290. doi:10.5502/ijw.v1i2.9

161 13 Moore 1981.

162 14 Heerwagen 1990.

163 16 Hartig, Mang et al. 1991, Cimprich and Ronis 2003, Berman, Jonides et al. 2008, Kaplan and Berman 2010.

164 ttp://www.prisonexp.org/ and https://en.wikipedia.org/wiki/Stanford_prison _experiment

165 Judith S. Beck. Questions and Answers about Cognitive Therapy. About Cognitive Therapy. Beck Institute for Cognitive Therapy and Research. Retrieved2008-11-21.

166 McCullough, M.E., S.D. Kilpatrick, R.A. Emmons and D. Larson: 2001, Is gratitude a moral affect?, Psychological Bulletin 127, pp. 249–266.

167 Watkins, P.C., K. Woodward, T. Stone and R.L. Kolts: 2003, Gratitude and happiness: Development of a measure of gratitude, and relationships with subjective well-being, Social Behavior and Personality 31, pp. 431–452.

168 McCullough, M.E., J. Tsang and R.A. Emmons: 2004, Gratitude in intermediate affective terrain: Links of grateful moods to individual differences and daily emotional experience, Journal of Personality and Social Psychology 86, pp. 295–309.

169 Emily L Polak, Michael E McCullough. Journal of Happiness Studies (2006) 7:343–360. Is gratitude an alternative to materialism?

170 Watkins, P.C., K. Woodward, T. Stone and R.L. Kolts: 2003, Gratitude and happiness: Development of a measure of gratitude, and relationships with subjective well-being, Social Behavior and Personality 31, pp. 431–452.

171 A study by Columbia Business School Professor Jonathan Levav, Class of 1967 Associate Professor of Business, Marketing and Professor Shai Danziger, Chairperson, Department of Management, Guilford Glazer Faculty of Business and Management, Ben-Gurion University of the Negev and Liora Avnaim-Pesso, a graduate student of Ben-Gurion University of the Negev, online in thenProceedings of the National Academy of Sciences(PNAS)

172 Sorrentino, R. M., Holmes, J. G., Hanna, S. E., & Sharp, A. (1995). Uncertainty orientation and trust in close relationships: Individual differences in cognitive styles. Journal of Personality and Social Psychology, 68, 314-327. http://dx.doi.org/10.1037/0022-3514.68.2.314

173 Kashdan, T. B., & Steger, M. F. (2007). Curiosity and pathways to well-being and meaning in life: Traits, states and everyday behaviours. Motivation and Emotion, 31, 159-173.

174 Burpee, L. C., & Langer, E. J. (2005). Mindfulness and marital satisfaction. Journal of Adult Development, 12, 43-51. http://dx.doi.org/10.1007/s10804-005-1281-6

175 Swan, G. E., & Carmelli, D. (1996). Curiosity and mortality in aging adults: A 5-year follow-up of the Western Collaborative Group Study. Psychology and Aging, 11, 449-453.

176 Brdar, I., & Kashdan, T. B. (2009). Strengths and well-being in Croatia. Unpublished raw data and Park N., Peterson C., & Seligman M. E. P. (2004). Strengths of character and wellbeing. Journal of Social and Clinical Psychology, 23, 603-619. http://dx.doi.org/10.1521/jscp.23.5.603.50748

177 Ranganathan VK1, Siemionow V, Liu JZ, Sahgal V, Yue GH.From mental power to muscle power--gaining strength by using the mind.

Printed in the United States
By Bookmasters